Dance Warrior

From Cancer to Dancer

Noelle Rose Andressen

Copyright © 2016 Noelle Rose Andressen

Front Cover Photo Copyright © 2014 Tim Agler
Back Cover Photo Insert Copyright © 2014 Jared Kale

All rights reserved.

ISBN-13: 978-0692666470 (Red Ribbons)
ISBN 10: 0692666478

DEDICATION

In the depths of my soul I search for one who deserves this place of honor. A place that will be immortalized as writing a book tends to do. The name of the person I choose must be done wisely and carefully, with purpose and meaning. I choose two people. The first: my son Jared Kale.

He tirelessly supported me when the skies grew dark and hope seemed distant. When I became tired and despondent of serving my dream, my mission, he would take my hand and tell me it would be okay.

He became my guide in dark places when I lost my sight. His hand first fit in my palm and now mine fits in his. Amazing how our children can grow right before our eyes and we only take notice of their bridge from child to adult at a seemingly appointed time ordained by fate and life's circumstances. You are a beautiful soul. Thank you, son! You have my heart.

…And for a beautiful butterfly who has yet emerged from her chrysalis. For you bfly…
In time we will both know why I chose you.

INTRODUCTION

To put pen to paper and write a book, any book, about anything, takes a certain amount of time, courage, and honesty. In having to be honest so I don't cheat you the reader out of a blessing or helpful hint, I need to be forthright in saying that I am an imperfect being. I do not have a perfect heart that makes decisions perfectly and I do not profess to know all the answers. I make mistakes, I lose patience, I lose my way, I lose hope, I lose strength, and I lose heart at times. I swear, I get afraid, I get weary, I get frustrated, I trip, I fall, and I also get back up and get going again.

With expression comes responsibility for that expression. Once the words are out there in the universe they gain momentum and life; whether good or bad. The outcome is seldom left for those intimately involved to decide. I believe in integrity as an artist and an author. One of the tenets I was taught was to be true to the facts, be true to yourself and be true to the emotions. However, some things are better left unsaid and some things that need to be said but will be unsaid. I have decided to state some things now and hope for another time when I can complete the truth with more perspective and understanding. For this reason I'm only choosing to reiterate main points that have to deal with my road to recovery after cancer. The rest that will remain unsaid at this time is a lovely tale about a rose and a butterfly. Their symbiosis is a bewildering and loving mystery.

Another note: While this is not a book about my cancer journey and what I went through at the clinic, I do reflect and reference some moments. I will at some point also put that story to paper in the form of a book, but those "heart-woundings" are still too fresh and I am not quite able to relive that journey in such specific detail in order to do it justice. I would be cheating you the reader, myself, and shortchanging the experience that deserves the attention in the proper timing.

Before committing this to paper, I pondered when to begin this story, it could've easily started with, January 10, 2006, ten years ago when I left the cancer clinic free from the disease, free from my cage. Another possible date is September 4, 2007 as that was when I was met by the most beautiful smile and most beautiful woman I'd ever seen. She would become my first ballet instructor in a very long time and would become the most important person to me on my rehabilitation journey post-cancer. I decided to start around that time. This was when I was enraptured by dance again.

September 6, 2007 was the day I chose to start my tale for reasons given herein.

This is about my journey after the cancer and how I put my life back together in the most unpredictable way one could have fathomed. How the weakest thing about me: my body, was used as a tool and a vessel to share love through dancing—my dancing. My goal is to give HOPE to those who may find themselves in a similar situation and place of destitution where they ask themselves, "Okay, now what?!" or for those who have shards of their lives laying on the ground before them in a huge jumbled mess. You can rebuild and be inspired by my steps. I dance and share my scars so that you will know that you too can heal.

So many today find themselves in this predicament of not knowing if they can regain all that was lost. Let my testimony do just that: encourage those that all that was lost can be regained; all can be reclaimed once again. Let me also add this: it may not be in the way you expect. I can attest that it will most likely be in the most unlikely way you could ever have imagined. I encourage you to take that grand journey and join me as I relive mine with you in these pages. I do HOPE that you will gain great encouragement and drive so that you too will want to endure life's challenges to reap the grandest benefits that this life can offer any of us. This too will be different for each one of us, but I promise you, that if you remain true to yourself and the love in your heart, incredible things can happen in your life. What seems to be a pile of mire or rubble can be made beautiful in due time.

I believe that good can triumph over evil ultimately. We just need more good men to do it. I'm only one person; more will be needed to turn many cold hearts around.

Do not be afraid to live your dream. Life doesn't offer receipts so you can't take it back. Spend wisely and live it well. You are the author of your life. Make it a best seller.

All my love, Noelle

PRAISES FOR DANCE WARRIOR - FROM CANCER TO DANCER

"I am overwhelmed by the beautiful vulnerability in this book by Noelle Andressen. Somehow I am able to relate to every word she writes. Noelle shows us that real strength comes from a conviction deep inside and the ability to appreciate the gifts she has been given in the face of all the odds against her following her dream. This book is a guaranteed inspiration." Alan Mercer/Celebrity Photographer

"A few years back, Noelle attended a contemporary dance workshop I was teaching in Los Angeles. Shortly she began attending my classes and was fully committed to the intense rigors of class. There never was any indication she was dealing with repercussions of cancer treatment. She never complained, shut down or gave up. At the same time Noelle was producing, choreographing and dancing with her own dance company Rubans Rouges Dance. She is a fighter, believer in dreams and a power house of positive energy. She's a petite red haired fire ball blasting through negativity wearing white angel wings. Noelle is a testament to a person who believes in following dreams no matter what obstacles are in the way. Never give up, never quit." Jamie Nichols / Dancer / Master Teacher / Choreographer / Executive Producer and Founder of Celebrate Dance

"Rich - inviting. A movement revolution with words. Noelle is a warrior and light to the arts community and the world." Sheila Garduna/ Writer

"Noelle's book Dance Warrior was such an inspiration. A reminder that all hope is never lost. Sometimes we just have to go back to the beginning and start again and again and again if we need to. Her candid sharing of her story is told in a way that we can all relate to with our own struggles in life and she does this in a way that makes you feel like you too can find what moves you and makes your heart sing. It is an uplifting story reminding us that is it never too late to dance or do what you love. Noelle is a woman who continues to beat the odds moving her life to its fullest and inspiring all who have the pleasure of knowing her. Having seen her story also told through dance I can honestly say that she is the full expression of hope and life and strength. Her artistic vision is uniquely her own and is a force. I was honored to see her perform and now to read her book. There is something in her words, her movement and her story for all of us." Salli Saffioti, Actress/Voice Over Artist

Taken only a few days after my mom passed. I could feel her embrace in the sunlight. © Jared Kale 2012

CONTENTS

	Acknowledgments	i
1	Back to the Beginning	1
2	So Much Guilt	15
3	Barnacles of HOPE	37
4	Beautiful Stranger	53
5	At the Shoreline	71
6	Life Begins where Fear Ends	89
7	Red Ribbons	107
8	Cancer to Dancer – Let This Be My Last Battleground	125
9	Six Weeks	177
10	Breathe	203
11	Dance Warrior	231
12	Cast Your Stone	259
	Conclusion	280
	Inspirational Notes	283

NOELLE ROSE ANDRESSEN

ACKNOWLEDGMENTS

I want to generously give my deepest thanks to many who helped me along my journey. It was a difficult one and in the beginning I often needed more than I gave. I have since remedied that and have given in return profusely.

My husband, Kristopher, you are a tireless warrior yourself. You remind me of a Greek god that has fierce power and strength that is unmatchable by many. You keep going no matter the odds against a situation.

I've not always been easy to be around during my healing but you stayed with me and gave from your heart, how and when you could. I love you as much as midnight loves the moon, and it is when you show your passionate and devotional love for God that I fall in love with you all over again. Your music that you create for me to dance to gives me such joy and lifts my feet from the earth so that I feel as if I am flying. This is how sublime your music is to me. You are my musical muse that sets my heart a flight and keeps my feet moving and my steps progressing. Music + Dance = the Perfect Marriage.

I would not be where I am now if it weren't for my mentors, teachers and dear friends. I've had many types of mentors in my life as I've worn many hats: a writer, screen writer, producer of many things in the entertainment world, singer, composer, actress, and currently and my most favorite – a dancer. Mentors and teachers, you all mean the world to me and will continue to guide my heart even though we may not be close in proximately any longer. These gifted human beings took their time with me in some way that pertained to dance. Whether it is technique, strength, stamina, creatively, educationally, production-wise, they all gave something different to me.

I also cannot forget the butterfly who remains in my heart as someone who is more than a mentor, and closer than a friend. You are more like family but that isn't even completely accurate and does not encapsulate it all. Then I ask: why explain the spiritual with simple words, for this goes beyond anything I can mortally explain with my words, but perhaps I can dance it for you.

I am older than some and younger than others. I mention this because I've been asked how I can be mentored by someone younger than me. I don't see people as an "age". I see everyone's hearts and souls as precious, with each having a special voice to share with the world. I can learn from anyone at any age of any age. We need to remember to be humble at all times and walk (or in this case dance) in grace and graciousness or we may miss a gift that God is trying to give to us through others.

My family and friends, colleagues, especially my best friend Sheila, who all saw my journey as perplexing but noble; I know you felt at times I was "silly" or "just dreaming", but I need to let you know that I deeply love you and appreciate all of your support no matter what you believed. That is a true testament to your character and love: you still loved me no matter what.

Tim Agler, for the beautiful photos you generously provided. Truly divine works of art. Thank You!

To my Nana. You were ultimately responsible for my dancing. You secretly taught me everything you knew and showed me how to perform like those beautiful actresses in the Golden Age of Hollywood. You gave me a love for cinema, dance, music, song, acting, and most of all God. It's hard to believe that you have been gone for eight years this St. Patty's Day. I think about you every day as there isn't a day that I'm not either dancing or watching dance.

Mom. You left soon after Nana. I still cannot wrap my mind around this departure. You died too young; too soon; too sudden. My footing has stumbled many times since. I don't fare well under this loss. I cannot explain this loss. I cannot forgive this disease that has taken all the strong women in my family and almost claimed me. For you, I dance for a cure for cancer. No one should lose another human being to this disease that takes everyone too soon.

My son. I already mentioned you in the dedication. You are my Samwise on this epic journey.

I choose to live whatever time I have left on this planet in beauty and gratitude for all everyone does for me. I have cherished every moment with each of you. I feel as though I have the better half of the experience by having been blessed to know you all. May I give back at least a small fraction of what was given to me.

NOELLE ROSE ANDRESSEN

CHAPTER 1
BACK TO THE BEGINNING
·· •♥ ə|ɓ ♥•··

"I would put my left hand to the ballet barre for the first time in years. It was September 6, 2007. . . I was going back to my beginning."

Cancer does not negotiate it does not discriminate, it shows no mercy. It can attack at any time without warning, it is no gentleman. It rapes, it robs, it destroys, it breaks bodies and hearts. Humanity has never known such a demon scourge as this. Noelle Andressen

NOELLE ROSE ANDRESSEN

Photo Jared Kale 2013

My grandmother, Marie, told me this when I was little, "If you ever lose your way, go back to the beginning." Ballet was my beginning as it was for hundreds of little girls. I can remember very little other than song, dance, movies and music from my youth. I clung to dance, particularly ballet. My grandmother also known as Nonna or Nana, as we were of Italian decent and from a large family, was a dancer and an actress that gave up her aspirations to raise her two beautiful daughters, my mother and my aunt. Nana was a passionate woman that spoke her mind and taught me how to do the same. She gave me my morals and showed me how to properly treat people.

My mom, whom I adore and will love forever, worked all the

time to support and raise my brother and me. It was a challenge but she rose to the occasion. She was very practical in not wanting my head to get stuck in a fantasy land. She wanted me to be prepared to have what she called a "real job" in administrative work. While I do thank her for being a realist as it was what supported my "art habit", I was not an administrator, I was an artist. We often butted heads over this because I wanted to dance, or sing, or act, etc. but we still loved each other. Our dad, was also amazing and gave us a lot and taught me how to survive in any circumstance. Since Nana was there mostly with her time for us, she was the one most influential in raising us.

Nana passed on what she knew to me including her love for dance, movies, and music. She showed me how to express myself through movement in our backyard. It was in the golden hour during sunset that she would speak to me about how dance would help heal her wounds and for a few moments feel free. "If you listen carefully to it, it will tell you how it wants to live in you. It is powerful. Use it for goodness. Let it lift you." From her words, I would often run to dance as a salve and use it for expression and to comfort me. I was hoping it would be there for me again in this process of healing from all that cancer had taken away from me.

At this point, having fought the good fight against cancer, I had nothing to lose and everything to gain. I had lost my way. I had lost my time. I had lost all my money. I had almost lost my life. There is a freedom in starting from zero. The numbers can only go up, however the feelings and experience of it all felt as if I was starting in the negative numbers.

September 4, 2007, I was 15 minutes early to a ballet class that I registered for at a community college across the street from my new home. I entered the hallway of a gym facility and managed to find my way. The halls smelled of cleaning chemicals and the noise of teenagers and early twenty-something's clamored about. In some cases I was almost old enough to be their parents and not too far away in age from the instructors themselves. I felt childish going backwards since I already had attained a BFA from UNLV, had a family, had a successful indie-film career, and danced on stage already.

It was an odd situation to go backwards but I did it for the purpose of regaining what I lost. I knew taking this dance class was what I had to do to get my body back into shape. Through this, I could re-learn to dance, repair my body, to love everyone, and figure out my life and what had happened. The rest, if there were to be anything more, would illuminate itself as I progressed. I had to trust in what I did not know and what I did not see.

I sat down on the floor like everyone else and we waited for the instructor to enter. This would be the day I met a beautiful stranger for the first time face to face. We had exchanged a couple friendly emails and neither of us knew much about the other or what we looked like. She waited until the last second before class was to start to appear. She was gorgeous and had an aura that was breathtaking. We read through the syllabus and asked questions about the course and were dismissed. My default was to leave the room without introducing myself, but I chided myself. The days of my shyness were over and I had a lot of healing from having been sexually abused as a child. Even though cancer took a lot from me and I was tempted to run, I forced myself not to behave like a hermit and not give into my fear of being hurt.

I went up to her, "Hi. I'm Noelle. I'm the one who emailed you a couple months ago." I said awkwardly to this beautiful woman who was now my dance instructor. "I'm just gonna have to fight harder than others."

"I'll help you fight." She said. With those words, I was completely unhinged and disarmed.

...*what is this? A kind heart who offered to help me— help ME to fight...*

It felt as if a thorn punctured my heart, as if love snuck in through my steel fortified walls and found a way in without warning and without my approval.

Continuously I kept thinking, "This was not in my plan. This was not supposed to happen." I had become accustomed to people wanting to destroy me. I just wanted to mind my own business and enjoy whatever time I had left on this planet and get my body in shape. I didn't want to get involved with anyone. At least that is what I thought and felt. I had too many "heart-woundings" at this point and very little to give. Then I noticed the beautiful stranger's smile shift slightly. While it truly was the most enrapturing smile that greeted me, there was also an underlying sorrow that I sensed from her; a pain behind the smile. I knew that there was a jewel beneath all of that strife begging to be freed. Perhaps she was a kindred heart who knew all too well what it felt like to be betrayed and pushed away.

Time would reveal truth in all of this for certain, as neither of us were ready for "THIS" or had planned for "THIS" at the time of our meeting. However all things are possible and made possible with HOPE. As you will see all things were in perfect sync with the universe's timing. Our being ready had nothing to do with it.

September 4, 2007 was a good day and date, even though it took me aback, but that would not be the correct day to use as my official start date back to dance—back to my beginning.

September 6, 2007 would serve as an official start-date benchmark and an altar of sacrificial beauty and love that would become clearer as the years progressed. There was only one reason why I chose this date because it had great significance.

I would put my left hand to the ballet barre for the first time in years on September 6, 2007. . . I was going back to my beginning. My hand connected to the metal and it was as if I could hear chains breaking and crumbling to the ground. It was more than a symbolic bondage that was broken. It was something in the spiritual realm that I could feel lifting from me like a dark cloak torn from my soul. That very action of just my placing my hand on that metal barre disrupted the evil that cancer was and how it tried to kill me. I was taking back all that was lost with that one simple action.

It was a humbling and awkward experience to be in a college class again because at this point in life as I shared, I already had my BFA and I had already had enough dance experience. It was a choice I made through determination and wonder. I was unsure if I could remember anything I had learned in all my years. I was incredibly nervous and felt out of place, something akin to trying on a formal gown ten sizes too large. I would have to re-grow into this beautiful garment called dance.

Fitting in was challenging, but most just didn't know where to place me relationally: sister, aunt, "mom"?! "Big Sister" worked for me and so it became known as my "role". They knew I was older, they knew I was married and we had a son, but how much older and experienced was not well discerned. This was not due to my trying to deceive, but out of protection, fearing that I'd be rejected due to my age, and that was an educated guess. I didn't want to face the same past adversities and desired beautiful relationships.

All the other students around me seemed familiar enough with this instructor, ballet and well poised with their hair pulled up in buns or tied back. Their leotards and tights were in perfect order. My hair was tousled in a messy pony tail and I was wearing some of the few clothes that I had owned: a black, spandex, midriff, top and black crop leggings. My attire was completely inappropriate for a ballet class. I was a mess. I knew I looked out of place but this was all I had. We left the cancer clinic with very little. We had sold our beautiful, ranch style home in Vegas to afford my treatment in order to save my life. We couldn't afford a nice place to live let alone afford a simple black leotard.

The instructor demonstrated a plié, I could feel my heart racing in my throat. My brain was still recovering having been besieged by all the toxins and chemicals from the cancer treatment that I couldn't remember the simplest things. When we had to execute the move, I had a panic attack. My muscles were trembling, I had a death grip on the barre, and I wanted to run out of that dance studio and forget my crazy notion. "What was I thinking? Getting back to dance again at my age?" I kept thinking this woman, my instructor, probably thinks I'm the most pathetic thing ever. I couldn't even plié properly, but the truth is, I could at one time.

At one time I was a decent dancer. It seemed so long ago. At that moment I had hated all that cancer and illness took from me. I wanted to scream "WHY?! Why me? Why did I have to lose so much?!" I loved dancing and it was lost to me. I couldn't even remember how to plié properly. Looking back, I think fear overwhelmed me to the point of my not being able to remember things. Fear can be extremely crippling if we let it be. It is only when we are completely free of fear that we are free indeed. It's fine to be afraid, just don't let it hinder you and your decisions. My

Nana (and one other) would tell me to do things anyway, even if I was afraid. I now tell you: Do it afraid if you have to. At that moment I reminded myself of this.

There I was, broken body, broken heart, broken mind; and yet I still went forward with my hands to the plow or in this case the barre, and I decided to never look back. I did that plié with the panic attack and I hoped my instructor wouldn't notice how bad my technique was. She did notice, and gave me a slight correction by moving my hand on the barre, it was too far back. I knew that, I just couldn't pull myself together to do anything correctly. I breathed through that one move and survived my first class. I was going to get through this one step at a time.

I came home like a grade school kid, full of wonder and joy peppered with some doubts and fear. I told my husband all that happened and how I was so thrilled to have the help of this woman. He marveled at how much I went on about her and was glad that I had felt well enough to complete one class. There were dozens more ahead as this was a college course. That was where my doubts and fears played on my mind. I doubted that I could finish what I started. The spirit was willing but unsure if the body was or if it would cooperate.

Our son jumped onto the couch and I squeezed him so hard. He was still very young at this time, a pre-teen. He never knew me, his mom, to be healthy as I spent his entire life ill. He was more excited than I was that I made it through my first class. He told me that he knew he'd see me dance sometime soon. For a little guy, he had more faith, more trust, more confidence, more discernment, than an adult twice his age.

When I finished sharing with the two men in my life, my husband and son, I looked outside my living room window. We lived directly across the street from the college that I was taking the ballet class. Incidentally, I had attended this college once before in my late teens. I couldn't help but notice how this seemed to come full-circle. What was my purpose here? Slight confusion and trepidation pricked at my humanity.

Just then, a little white butterfly flew in front of our glass window pane. It was as if it wanted me to pay attention to it so it could tell me a tale. Butterflies were never something I was fond of. I paid little attention to them in the past, but since my cancer treatment, I had been seeing them more than I could remember. I opened my heart up to these little tissue paper like creatures with wonder and curiosity. What was it about these things that I found myself suddenly drawn to? I watched this one fly around the window for a few moments before it soared away.

The way it flew away caused me to think about the metamorphosis it had taken to get to this stage in its life. The connection between me and it was a parallel for a new start or possibly a re-birth. Even though I had gone back to my beginning to find my footing and to find my way, I knew I wouldn't be repeating the same pathway my life had taken prior to cancer.

Something in the back of my mind told me that I was in for the journey of a life time.

I would learn in time that it was not for the sake of the dance alone that I would begin dancing again. There was another calling on my heart: to shed bitterness, to bring good news of joy, to share my story, to love someone, or perhaps several "someone(s)" unexpectedly and to bloom and grow. I was now a Rose and this was the garden in which I was to be planted in. This beautiful stranger now in my life reminded me of a butterfly. In my mind I saw her as such: a butterfly. A lovely dancing butterfly, and referred to her as one: "b-fly".

These things would not be made fully apparent to me at the start except for little signs along the way that would flutter past my cheek, whispering sweet promises of good things to come. These good things couldn't even possibly be imagined nor conjured up in my own mind, for I was unable to trust and love in the current broken state that I had arrived in.

Then that night, before I fell to sleep, I realized that I was, this scared, little red-headed, dancer with gifts from above: love and empathy. After my having been so wounded, ill, scared, lost, I had found myself immediately won over by the kindness and compassionate words from this instructor. It was nourishment to my soul. Even more than that, I couldn't help to think about her beautiful smile and how I could sense something sullen beneath it.

I considered that my purpose there was to be someone to help guide her. It seemed odd to me because I was the one in need.

Perhaps I was in need but not in the way anticipated. Perhaps we were both in need. For the law of nature can be fickle and have a duality to it: to love your enemies as you would love yourself. It also would serve as the true test to break open a heart, to prove love for others and yet be conflicting at the same time. I have to be honest and share that I begged the powers that be that night to not let what was ahead be painful. I had had enough of that already. I had too much loss, too much pain, too much to bear. I had little to give anyone let alone be a guide for someone, for that was what I felt floating in my heart like a lost message at sea.

If only I knew at that time that my being there just wasn't for me. It was as if when I placed my hand on that barre, September 6, 2007 a beautiful light of love shone in my life. All I wanted to do was dance, but there was another purpose for me.

CHAPTER 2
SO MUCH GUILT

"Don't cry over anything that can't cry over you." Marie Cutrona

There is a guilt that brings about death and a guilt that leads to freedom. However, false guilt can be the cruelest of all; neither having been earned by deed or alleviated by repentance. You must heal from the past so you can have a future. Noelle Andressen

If you've done wrong, your conscience will eat at you until you make it right no matter what you do. Be careful beloveds, the stains of wrong doing don't wash off so quickly. A clear conscience rests easy. Oh the weight of the poor soul who goes to bed with a guilty conscience. Noelle Andressen

Las Vegas home at Christmas time in 1995

Slam! Bang! Screech!

This was what my family and I heard on a daily basis living in our new apartment. Very little sleep was had. Seldom was it more than a couple hours of consistent, quiet rest.

Every night before we went to bed, I would lie on the mattress and stared up at the ceiling. I wondered what would drive me to frustration or scare me to death each night. "Honey, what is that on the ceiling? Is that the upstairs plumbing leaking again or a bug?" My husband had a bug towel and a water towel ready for action.

It didn't take long for us to realize we were living in a wretched place. The neighbors upstairs constantly making noise, the other neighbors in the complex throwing rowdy parties, but what was worse were the robberies, the murders, the drug dealings, creepers and peepers, the meth lab in the same apartment complex, rapes, and every crime imaginable occurring in the neighborhood and on the college campus across the street.

Dear friends of ours, a sweet middle aged couple, visited our place the first few months we lived there. She was a retired counselor and he was a retired parole and probation officer from Vegas. As they were leaving they gazed at the artwork on the back wall of our complex where we parked our vehicle. He identified all the markings to be graffiti gang symbols. He knew them all by name and it was not Picasso, Van Gough or Da Vinci. He warned us to get out of that place as soon as we possibly could. It was not a good neighborhood at all.

This was the last thing I needed to hear. He meant well, but I had already felt so much guilt for having to sell our beautiful 4 bedrooms, 3 bathroom, ranch style home to pay for the cancer treatments. Upon hearing his words of warning again, it made my heart crumble.

"What were we doing here? Was my life truly worth this much in loss? Why did my family have to suffer so much because of me? Maybe I should have just let myself die so they wouldn't have this burden? They had to live in this horrid place because of me." I thought quietly. We were only meant to live in that place for a short time, it was a transition place, but truth be known, we would live in that place for 10 years.

Unbeknownst to everyone that knew me, the nights ushered in great tears of regret. I literally counted the nights we had to spend in this place. On night #109 the same thoughts stirred like a beast that couldn't be satiated or defeated. I was suffering from guilt--false guilt.

That night I reflected back. Thoughts of how our home looked during the winter Holidays flooded my heart. I saw visions of our beautiful home with all the dreamlike decorations, mistletoe, large delicate snowflakes that hung from the cathedral ceiling in the great room and stunning white columns that accented the overhangs. It was a gorgeous winter wonderland every year at that time.

This was not only a home, it was a living, breathing, continuous work of art. It was an artistic expression that we lived in and created. The art of the home was the heart of the home. It too became a soul-collaboration like most of our other work as husband and wife.

The vast, great room was a combination of my husband's and my love for European culture. I designed the intricate floor pattern that was an eclectic modern-Roman style with tumbled, Italian, marble tile in an earthy terra cotta color with creamy white borders. He laid down the tile with his own hands. The grand archway from the great room into the dining room was my favorite. It had the Italian word for HOPE: "esperanza" carved out of maple wood hanging above it. It was literally our "Arch of Hope". We decided as a family we would never lean on our own understanding but rest upon the greater shoulders of "HOPE". On my worst health days, this would prove to be a savior.

This portico was very transporting and felt like the outdoors coming indoors. It was a merging of old world European with a dash of contemporary design. The walls were textured plaster and painted with soft neutrals. The kitchen was where my husband's culinary craft kicked in and many incredible meals were prepared.

Most of the rest of the home was like this with secret nooks of memories artfully displayed.

Our son had, at that time, spent all but 8 months of his little life in that home. It was filled with his "firsts". His first steps, words, songs, dances, major "owies", all of it were in this home. The archway wall with pencil markings chronicled his growth and the backyard had his treehouse like swing set that became the playing field of his imagination. When I was ill and couldn't go outside or play with him, I would sit on the chaise and watch him play out his stories. My little prince would go on to become a strong, true-life warrior in ways that only can be whispered in sleep as dreams often do. So much delight and joy was found in our backyard.

A huge bay-window extended from the dining room and overlooked the side yard. You could recline like goddess on the cushions that I made and fall asleep basking in the sun. A lot of momentous instances happened in that area of our home. One was a romantic interlude with my husband the other was a morose cry with my grandmother. This was where Nana first wept in my arms and told me that she didn't feel well. She was sick. She had cancer.

A happier occasion occurred when I had planned a "Family Encouragement Party". The goal was to bring our fractured extended family into an alignment of love. My assignment for every family member: Write down three positive things about each member in the family, come to our home, read those things while looking into their eyes, and enjoy some amazing desserts that I made. The party went well, we all felt the love in the room, and for a time my family of ten was in perfect harmony.

There were other warm memories with family and close friends and also some intense moments and deep "life scars" that made and shaped the character of "me".

We had to either give away or sell most of our belongings to pay for my treatment. My sorrow was on behalf of our son who gave up and lost the most things like his toys but would later be replaced, for my husband who lost his electronics and man cave devices and for myself who lost mostly clothes and sentimental items. We kept our musical instruments one computer, and one bed. This purging and casting away was difficult to do. It left gapping scars in me and I think my family in some ways.

It was a traumatic experience that shaped all of us. For the most part I chose and still choose to remember the positive and use the hardships and challenges as a means to encourage others and as a benchmark to see how far I have come in my journey.

Much like extravagance to a blind man is foolishness, I often chastised myself as I felt I was being foolish dwelling upon the materialistic things of the past because I had survived a life threatening disease. I should be satisfied with surviving. I was not. This was a deep wounding. This was going to take a lot of "soul work" to heal from. I had to heal from my past so I could have a future. Our pasts can be unnecessary anchors. We must heal that burden and travel lighter as we move forward. There have been several occurrences in my life where this notion would be put to the test.

My grandmother's distant but soothing voice in my head would remind me, "Don't cry over anything *(or "anyone", my addendum)* that can't cry over you." She would also add if the tears kept falling, "Tears aren't a sign of weakness. They're the soft revving of the heart gearing up in mighty strength that's about to break forth." I would tell myself that it was "just" a house, but the oceans of my loss would fall down my cheek any way. My mom had given us the down payment for our home. It was supposed to be our security. It would have been paid off at this current date.

To say I suffered from extreme guilt would be a gross and ironic understatement. It was a pain that I hadn't experienced before and one that would rival the anguish I felt when my mother and grandmother died from cancer. The anguish wasn't because I personally lost my home, although there was a bit of that as well, the anguish was mostly there because I felt I caused so much loss for my family and dreams of our son growing up in a beautiful home near his friends and extended family in a lovely neighborhood were gone. It was all gone. It was my entire fault.

So there I was, this one particular night, suffocating from

regretful tears, when I got out of bed in our current apartment and went into the kitchen. It was extremely dinky and it wouldn't take more than the moonlight peeking in through a gap in the curtains to send the roaches scurrying, or in this case my opening the refrigerator door that caused the light to come on. We had an unopened bottle of wine that looked tempting, very tempting, I decided against it—this time, and grabbed a glass of water instead and sat on the couch in the living room.

Sleep escaped me, inner peace aloof, and the future a questionable entity that teased. Peace from guilt was what I wanted. Wholeness was what I begged for. Perspective was based on the truth of how I felt at that instant instead of factual truth that could be proven. The truth is, I felt that I could never regain anything that was lost but had a determination to try. I still don't know where this determination came from. It was most likely based on the deeply seeded teachings of my Nana who was a strong God-fearing woman that was not flawless and embraced her frailties. She often reminded me, "If those around you try to hide your light, they're only afraid of your brilliance reflecting on their mediocrity."

Through the kitchen window, I saw the sun coming up as it crested over the treetops. The dimly lit college campus could be seen through many of our front room windows. With a cup of tea in hand, I contemplated how found myself on this new, grand, adventure back to dancing with a beautiful stranger guiding me, "the b-fly". She was very accomplished, had impressive credits and background. Her dancing was inspiring, at least it was to me. There was a maternal presence about her but it wasn't only due to her age; there was a deep compassionate heart that wanted to express and give so much. I doubt many if any ever knew or saw that in her. I saw it and wanted to learn more about her and offer whatever I had to help heal any brokenness.

As the days and weeks under her tutelage passed, I could see a forced air of being 'put together" and elegance portrayed by her, but I knew it was more than that. There was a human heart of flesh inside of her that needed to be set free. A heart that could tell many stories of adversity but maybe not triumph, not yet, that would still be forthcoming. Sometimes the heartstrings of humanity play songs that have discord and sometimes harmony. I found myself caught in this chaotic melody that was intriguing and bewildering. Despite that, she inspired me to continue my dance pursuit and I did. I worked very hard, got to class early, practiced all the time, asked questions, and tried to find the nuances in her detailed teachings and physical presentation.

One day for class I took the time to put my hair up in a crown braid instead of my messy, 1980's, high ponytail. Often, I felt that braids were one of the most feminine expressions for women's hair, a perfect match for ballet.

"The b-fly" would wear her long hair in a French Braid down her back and it was exquisite. Without her saying so, I got the hint that she preferred hair worn in the ways she did hers: French braid, bun, and a few other elegant styles, so I did this for her to show how thankful I was for her help. As she passed besides me at the barre, I saw a pleased smile cross her face. I briefly smiled back. I deduced that she was sincerely glad to see me employ classical classroom ballet etiquette. She didn't require or ask for this adherence, but it did please her. This exchange was so delightful but would be short lived.

Since braiding was an ordeal for me because of the autoimmune like symptoms in my hands, the braiding only happened this one time. It was difficult for me to maneuver my fingers to do this finite weaving. The next time we had class, I went back to my messy ponytail and I could tell she was disappointed in me for she didn't smile at me at all. In one sense I couldn't blame her because she sincerely was pleased with my progressing in the finite details of the art of ballet, however, I could not physically do it continuously much like my not being able to remember more than 2 counts of 8 of choreography. I disappointed her like an unruly child and my false guilt about selling our home to save my life flooded in. This was a trigger for me that I had to be aware of and mend.

A few times I can recall "The b-fly" mentioning how she was seen as a "mom", not a dance mom, but a mother figure to many of these younger adults and teens. Could she think I was that young? I wasn't. I also wasn't seeking a "mother figure". I already had a real mother and if you included my Nana I had two. I had already gone through the wounding in the church setting under the wings of a "spiritual mother", the last thing I wanted was another "mother-daughter" relationship to fail. Was this to be just a friendship, maybe? I didn't believe I could currently offer that in my devastation. My heart's motto: "No one else in, No one else out." That was my wall. It was my fortress to defend and keep strong. However, I would find myself doing otherwise, for I was compelled. Compelled to only allow this one in, but only this one and no more I convinced myself. The word "compelled", had significant meaning to me. It had such strength and drive and action that paralleled with it; and so I let her in a little at a time.

On "good days", she was helpful and open to exchanges with me. On "not so good days", there was a wall much like mine that was a solid metal citadel. I recognized it as past wounds creating a safety around the flesh heart encased in stone. I knew this because I could recognize it in me. We tend to detect in others what is also in or was in ourselves; and interestingly, this caused an unexplainable connection between us.

This was the strangest oddity: I could always sense her presence before I saw her or knew that she was near me. I tended to think it was the same way for her as there was that "something" that drove us together and at times that same "something" pushed us apart. When two passionate hearts collide, without intention, the very force that draws them together can also propel them apart. There can be great comfort in knowing that, at least it was the case for me.

It was time to work on the combination center floor. I dreaded this part because of my memory issues and it triggered frustration. Knowing the steps in your heart reveals the passion, knowing the steps in your head reveals the technique. My memory was a battle I'd rather not have had to fight. This one particular day I just couldn't get the get the steps correct. I could tell "The b-fly" was losing patience with me, but I couldn't force my body to do what I wanted it to do. I attempted the combination again and my legs were trembling slightly.

We were doing a very simple pas de bourree and during the plié with the coupe I lost my balance and stumbled; she saw me stumble. Never having been known for poor balance or two left feet in my entire life, after cancer I had more left feet than a millipede. Letting "The b-fly" down was embarrassing and that day I convinced myself that I had been a great disappointment. A subtle look of disdain from her and then ignoring me for the rest of class reinforced my feelings. I quietly left class and walked home. I couldn't help but think she hated me.

I laid on the wooden floor in our living room and stared up at the water stained ceiling. I wanted to give up. I wanted to stop and run away, it was too hard. What once was easy was extremely hard. At that point I was about to quit, but then dancing lights sparkled and moved on the ceiling.

Car headlights passed our windows and shone brightly on the white plaster canvass over me. It reminded me of a segment in the Disney film Fantasia. Dance beckoned me at that instant, I stood on my feet and began to recall the movements from earlier that week in class. My feet seemed to remember the way more than my heart or head but they all conflicted constantly and took turns at creating a hindrance. This garment was still frustratingly too large for me to adorn with style and emotion. Had I truly lost it all? Sorrow set in quickly.

After falling asleep in the living room I woke up on the couch and it had all seemed like a dream. Upon looking out the window, the school reminded me that it was far from a dream and was my reality. Determined, I got up again and began working on the combination, I just couldn't make it happen. Left was right and right was left. My body ached, my heart sank and tears flowed. My husband came into the room, "I need your help." I said pitifully.

"I don't know anything about dancing." He left the room. This wasn't the truth. He did know about dancing, we met dancing on stage at the Bob Hope McCallum Theatre. We both danced a lot together while we were dating. "Really, I need your help." I called down the hall to him. "You just don't want to."

"You'll figure it out for yourself. It'll pass."

"Please I need your help. Encouragement, something. You have no idea what I'm going through. Any time I have to fight you run away, just like you did at the clinic." All my resentment poured out and as soon as I heard my own outspoken voice I cringed knowing that I had said something regrettable. Several rounds of the blame game lasted for about an hour.

Many harsh words were spoken between us and I was broken,

even more. While I may have been right, my timing was off. This would be a lesson that I would learn later on in a more severe way. My passion, honesty, truthfulness, and my mouth got the best of me as it usually did then.

After my pleading tears, my husband finally said to me, "Dance from your heart not your head." I understood these words. These were the words of the man I fell in love with. He only made occasional appearances lately. When moments like this would happen over the many years of our marriage, I would savor them like sweet morsels and also felt like I was hit by a bitter dart. The duality was difficult to abide in until eventually I gave up on the man that I emotionally lost and accepted it. (The depths of this will be saved for another book.) Even still, he had wisdom. Once I yielded to what he said, I was able to succeed. I was so thrilled I had to share this with another. An email exchange between my "The b-fly" and I ensued:

"Sat 10/13/2007 12:15 PM – I Finally Got It!
Sorry I messed up that last dance combination. Another student stayed with me after class a few minutes to help me with the arms, but the feet were still a problem. I practiced for 5 hours when I got home and still couldn't do it. My husband watched and he said "dance from your heart not your head." I cried it out for a few minutes and then I did the steps just fine. I felt really stupid, but what he said just clicked. Now I just gotta put feet and arms together. Thanks, for pushing me, few have cared enough to do so. Noelle"

She thanked me for sharing and encouraged me to keep the

joy. It was written so beautifully. I had a difficult time understanding how she seemed to be very upset with my failure in class but then write something this beautiful to me. The apparent contradiction told me that there was something underlying there but at that time I chose not to inquire. (While I worked on this book I re-read her emailed words several times and to this day they still bring great comfort.) Her words then inspired me to visit an old friend called "Choreography". I kept this in the back of my mind.

The brush fires in the autumn of 2007 were fierce and marred the Los Angeles skies with charred clouds. The air quality was greatly affected and I never fared well under conditions like this. I had suffered with mitral valve prolapse for a few years prior to the cancer. It caused many additional symptoms like fatigue, heart palpitations, migraines, lightheadedness, etc. I had some problems and symptoms exacerbated when I started dancing again especially in the smoggy Los Angeles air when the conditions were less than perfect. During this fall season the brush fires caused my heart valve condition to worsen under it. It caused heaviness on my chest and sometimes shortness of breath.

Class was still in session during Southern California's urgent situation. I didn't want "The b-fly" to see my labored breathing and thought I hid it well until after class. I sat down and rubbed my chest. It was odd though because the pressure was in a different location that it usually was when I had MVP symptoms. The compression was felt where the "thorn" had slipped in. Of course this was a figurative event but at that time I began to wonder if there was more to it than just an expression of speech.

I stood up and hid behind one other student hoping to slip out of the classroom unnoticed. It was a trifle incident and I knew exactly what to do: get into a warm shower and stay in the bathroom for a while until the smoky air cleared some. If it got too bad, we would have to leave the city for a time. I sighed relieved that I had escaped the dance studio without event until I heard my name called. It was "The b-fly" and she noticed. I didn't want to involve her at all so I told her it was nothing, but as events developed and she learned more she asked that I get a doctor note to clear my medical condition. She seemed earnestly concerned about me, and that touched my heart, at least this is what I told myself, however, there were some things that occurred later in the future that made me question this.

I won't go too much into this accept to say that it played an incredible role in fate and was a piece to a miracle. I chose to not delve into this at this time because it is a sensitive subject for both of us. Out of love and respect, I won't attempt to go into the details about it in this book. Perhaps this is something that she and I will write together one day, or maybe it will be left unsaid. As for now, I find it appropriate just to briefly mention it as it is integral to the miraculous element of my story.

We didn't have hot water at our apartment, couldn't afford it, so I had to settle for a cold shower to help soothe my symptoms.

Something about the cold, it made things hard and almost impenetrable. The past experiences at our former church rushed forward and overwhelmed me with thoughts I hadn't dealt with in a long time. When healing from cancer the worst thing to do is get upset as it lowers your immune system. I took in deep breaths and let the droplets sooth me. While there was past friction with my former pastor's wife, and where I place responsibility for the spiritual damage I received while in church, she often had wise words to say. Not all was tarnished and not all was lost. She told me that when I felt so beaten down and not sure what to do, that is the time that I should give, even if I give out of my need.

Yes, of course, I "should" give something to someone. Giving a gift would be my next step in my journey. I would create a dance for my husband as a way to say thank you for standing by my side during my cancer trial and a desperate attempt at repairing a damaged relationship. A myriad of wonderful dance moves and ideas flooded in my head and my own smile penetrated and enlightened my soul. Nervous as I was to inquire with "the b-fly" about my idea especially after the exchange in the hallway, I took a deep breath and followed through by contacting her.

"Thursday 11/1/2007 10:48 PM – Dance Room

Couple of questions: Can I use the dance room before class, if yes, what is an ok time? And can I bring a CD player, I won't put it too loud. I'd like to choreograph something for my husband. I'm not good at this--it'll be a challenge, but I want to give him a special gift for sticking with me through the hardships. He was the only one that believed I'd be dancing again, even I didn't believe it.

I hope I did all right today. I tried to be myself and let my personality come out a bit. I'm not comfortable doing that...not yet...I don't know if you can understand, but cancer took more away from me than I'd like to admit. On the other side of success I feel as if I live with a silent disease inside of me, waiting to appear again and rip the things that I love away. It makes me hesitant in all that I do, I have a hard time connecting w/ people, being myself...sorry, thanks for listening. I'll see you soon and thank you for all that you do. Noelle

My words were very sobering to me as I re-read them before sending it out. Cancer **was** the silent disease inside of me, possibly waiting to explode again. It was something I tried not to think about. It was something that although my family knew was a strong probability, I didn't want them to dwell upon it. If it would try to attack me again, I was prepared with more knowledge for the next time. I would not allow myself to end up in bed. My doctor in Vegas advised me about that. He told me it's good to rest when needed, care for yourself, but don't stay in bed unless absolutely necessary. Even in hospitals they got patients up on their feet as soon as possible. If I met this internal enemy within again on my battlefield, I would remember this well. With that thought, I hit "send" and waited. She was prompt with her reply.

She gave me permission to use the studio before class to create a dance for my husband. She added that choreographing for someone I loved sounded like a positive step and hoped that I would find peace in this.

At that moment, after reading her words, my heartstrings were touched deeply. I had thought she hated me for letting her down so much. I was wrong. With such beautiful words I wondered if she too enjoyed writing and communicating the way I did. Her words hinted at a deep, understanding, soul, for who could truly say these things without something substantive behind them. They would have collapsed under the weight of falsehood. Based on our interaction in class and our exchanges, I believed something special was developing. I had a strong respect and admiration for this woman and was grateful for her in my life. With her words, I was energized to do anything and I knew that I could. At that time my knowing that someone believed in me or at least wanted to help was a very powerful thing. She wanted to help me, at least it came across to me that way, otherwise why facilitate my request.

It was official, this would be my next step into the world of dance. I kept creeping forward at a fast pace unbeknownst to me at that time that these were the steps back into performing and then performing professionally.

The computer screen started to blur, my vision was dimming and a rainbow like arc crested over my right eye. A blind spot covered more than half of my field of vision, I could no longer read "The b-fly's" email. I put my hands to my head and covered my eyes as my head started to throb. I felt light headed and thought I'd pass out. I didn't and my vision slowly returned. I laid down in bed and massaged my temple. My doctors warned me that I could experience post cancer treatment symptoms, I shrugged it off and categorized it as such.

My eyes closed and I thought "The b-fly's" words. "Someone I love…find peace" This message encouraged and also alarmed me, "Choreography for someone you love…" *Someone I love??!* Little did she know that my love for my husband was tattered, barely functioning, barely breathing. My husband and I both knew the courageous and noble thing was to fight for our marriage and stand true to our vows that we pledged. The cancer fight wasn't only for my life but also a fight for our relationship. More guilt compiled and it wasn't my dance or "The b-fly's" fault. She had no idea what irony she had treaded upon, or did she? Strong ties between the two of us were already beginning to form back then. Could she read my pain as much as I could read hers?

CHAPTER 3
BARNACLES OF HOPE

"Our hope must be like a barnacle and cling to all that's good."

Dance is the heartbeat in which my soul resonates to. Music is the carriage in which it sojourns; to leave behind heart imprints embedded on the stage of humanity...and thus I dance...and thus I HOPE. Noelle Andressen

The last time we saw Nana was in November 2007.

Hope. What an ominous and mysterious word. HOPE. The messages from "The b-fly" caused me to seriously contemplate and question where I had placed my peace which was a product of hope. When did I lose it, and how can I find it again? The answer to, *"I survived cancer, now what?!"* had a short term goal attached to it: create a dance for my husband. That was all I needed to focus on at the moment, but the reality was that my mind was scattered and worried about my bond with my husband being strained and the what if's. What if I cannot do this? What if he doesn't like it? What if he doesn't get what I'm trying to say to him?

During that time, when either of us spoke we collided harshly and intense rounds of arguments that led to fights ensued. We were both sensitive and emotionally raw from the experience at the clinic. We were drained from having to combat cancer like a World War veteran suffering from post-traumatic stress syndrome. It had tested us beyond what we had faced previously, something that I don't feel any couple should have to face. There are enough troubles in our world that did and would still barrage us and other families; fighting an enemy such as this seemed crueler than what humans should have to deal with.

The final outcome that we survived was unbelievable. Even with all of this against us, we both had love in our hearts to want to try and that made all the difference.

For him, he chose a path of patience that was not always executed with perfection. He tended to run away and anesthetize himself with "anything" that would allow him to avoid facing the truth. His "drug of choice" was negligence. This was the weakness in his character that had plagued him often.

For me, I chose to convey my thoughts and emotions with dance. My mouth was a double edged sword that spoke the truth and would edify others and set them free, but it could also hurt with its piercing drive, this was my weakness. With dance, I could get my ideas across without my big mouth to mess it up or his reaction to those words to break my heart. (At this current time, we have both greatly improved and have a union that is strong and respectful.)

My next ominous question: After this dance, what next? I couldn't see a future. I didn't know how to heal my past or my relationship with my husband but was attempting to do so with dance.

At that point I could only think about God in the physical and not the spiritual because of my anger. I was furious at God for allowing so much loss and so much hurt to come into my family's life; this wasn't part of the plan. It never was. Now we had a huge mess and I felt abandoned and forgotten with it on my shoulders.

Knowing where your footing is in this world helps to navigate it. My footing was challenged and I was knocked off my center. I had to place my HOPE in something greater than dance and greater than myself so I could have peace.

Yet, our HOPE must be like a barnacle and cling to all that's good. We must place our trust in something seen or unseen. The only thing I could think of that was purely good in this world was God. I chose to cling to God for the moment. I felt Him pushing me to dance and create a dance. With that I took a deep breath and held it in. I placed my hand on my heart, it was beating. Even in the stillness of breath there is life. Upon that acknowledgment I exhaled and with determination I stood up.

"Let's just start with these small steps first." I told myself but not seriously thinking anything else would come of these first small steps.

When my husband went to work I would secretly craft this dance gift for him. Excitement and frustration were my silent partners and joy and sorrow ran the race alongside me. The steps came out wrong, my execution of them limited, my body nowhere near what it used to be, I was a living echo of my past, haunted by photos of greatness in my memory. What I wanted to do and what I could do were very opposite things at that time. I lost most of my mobility, flexibility, knowledge, courage, and strength. All I had at that time was a willingness to do it, and that made all the difference.

It became very dizzying to war with my desire and the factual reality. I would put the music on and try again and again to make something cohesive; anything that would work. It just wasn't working and I wasn't even sure what I was trying to say to my husband. Why were the steps not coming out? Why couldn't I communicate with my movements? Why was I so terrible? Had I truly lost it all? Why don't I just give up this is a silly and absurd notion any way. However, sometimes you have to walk on the brink of absurdity to discover a moment of genius; or in my case I'd settle for some half way decent choreography.

With that, I realized what was in the past had to stay there and I had to move on. I recalled what my beloved dance instructor said to me upon numerous occasions. I was starting from scratch and indeed another complete beginning. The reality of what I had lost never sank in so harshly. I lost my health, I lost my home, I lost my dancing, I lost everything except my family.

I went to our computer and I re-read "The b-fly's" email. My eyes swelled up with tears. I tried to choke them down but just as soon as that thought occurred to me, the wetness burst and escaped down my cheeks.

"Someone I love…find peace in all this." Her words hit me harder the second time I read them. A sense of peace?! She had no idea what I was struggling with, or so I thought, trying to convince myself that this beautiful woman would not penetrate my heart. She actually hit my heart precisely where the target was: at my reality—my truth. *Darn it, how did she know this about me? I thought I hid it so well.* She was correct though, I needed to find a sense of peace about it all…somehow.

This dance was a love gift for my husband, I needed to focus on that and not the technique of the steps or the execution of the steps. I had to let go of what I lost and stop grappling for it so I could embrace what was presenting itself now. I needed to release and heal the past so I could have a future, a future with my husband that would be grounded in a deeper love than before the cancer.

Since I'm never one to let myself feel self-pity or sorrow, I gave myself the ten minute grieving window I often permitted for myself. Then I picked myself up again and began creating some absurd movements knowing I probably wouldn't use any of it, but I had to press forward and break out of my self-inflicted jail cell. It was all going to be different this time around with my dancing. Cancer made me a new person much like going from a caterpillar to a butterfly. The very thing that causes the caterpillar to die, is the very thing that cause the butterfly to fly. Yet somehow, love finds a way to open doors and the window of our hearts unlocked.

The air of freedom let in so we can finally breathe.

With a few abstract pieces of choreography I was able to come up with a dance phrase. It was not my best work but it was something to springboard off of.

After about an hour re-working choreography, stretching, and conditioning, I collapsed onto the couch by the window. This new dance and the ballet class were extremely challenging for my little framed body and I was still dealing with recovering from my treatment including other ailments. I was exhausted. The next day I would be able to test out my choreography in the dance studio at the college. I pulled the burgundy curtains aside and watched the light breeze traipse through the mulberry tree branches.

A flying shadow caught my eye. I wondered if it was a friendly, fluttering visitation in the midst of a Southern California autumn. It was. A monarch butterfly made an appearance and did a brief airy dance, perhaps my interpretation of a little bow, and flew swiftly away. Its presence gave me a sense of HOPE. Something I hadn't felt in quite a long time. Not even surviving cancer instilled this in me. It took the words of a beautiful stranger and infinitesimal appearances of butterflies as subtle reminders of beautiful transformations yet to come to get me to have HOPE.

I had never paid much attention to butterflies, and can't recall seeing them in my youth but I must have seen them as I grew up in the Garden State of New Jersey where flowers were in abundance. I wasn't a prissy girl on the inside, but I loved dance and I loved sports, I just did it all in dresses and matching hair bows. I even shunned seeing butterfly or rose printed anything in our home, it just wasn't for me. In my adulthood I found myself captivated by these dainty creatures and had a change of heart towards them and roses almost instantly after the cancer.

My face creased with a huge smile as I sat up to see if I could possibly catch another glance of it. It was gone, but the school was there in my sight and sullenness quickly replaced my joy. *Why does my heart sink when I look at it?*

It was perplexing to think about how and why we found ourselves living across the street from this institution. I was an Emmy nominated screenwriter, producer, and musician. Living here and going back to school was absurd; not thinking with prideful intention but it weighed heavy upon my heart that it was no accident—it had to have purpose and meaning; something I didn't understand yet. I've come to believe that there are no coincidences. I do think that our lives are masterfully shaped like a potter with the clay.

All things in life no matter how insignificant they may seem to us, have intention and purpose. Each of our actions and reactions cause others to respond and react when certain chain of events unfold and options present themselves. One slight variation or deviation can change a multitude of elements in our lives. Turning left instead of right can mean the difference of saving someone's life or taking it, no matter how unintentional our intentions are. I've learned since to tread carefully.

I rested my chin on the back of our couch and contemplated

what this all meant on the grand stage called the universe. I knew what I felt in my heart, I knew what I wanted to do short term, I knew I had to because I was compelled. What exactly was compelling me? I could not tell you or anyone at that time, I had this anchor in my heart that I'd rather not have had. I wanted to travel lightly and this was a daunting burden that showed no mercy. My broken body was so weakened, dancing was so difficult.

I also didn't want any new heart connections, I didn't want to risk trusting anyone or loving anyone, mostly out of fear of being hurt again and then also not knowing if I would live long enough to enjoy any other relationships.

"Best not to get too involved." I told myself but what we want, what we desire doesn't always make sense or are not tangible things that we understand and adhere to.

We can start things for one reason and finish them for other reasons; or as Forest Gump said, "Sometimes we just do things that don't make any sense." This may be one of those things. As I said: I was compelled to go forward and do what I was doing.

This instructor, this woman, this beautiful stranger, "The b-fly" was in my life whether I liked it or not. She presented to me (most likely unknowingly) something I didn't want to face or deal with: myself. I didn't want to let anyone in and yet the thorn in my heart that slipped in the first day I met her was throbbing and caused me to let her in against my will.

Peace? How did she know about my lack of peace. Did it show? Did I give it away too easily in my emails? Why did I trust her?

Why did she trust me? Why did she care so much? Why didn't I push her away like I did everyone else?

At last, this is where I dragged a spiritual God into the equation when he should've been dragged into it at first.

I called out to God, "Why have you brought me here to this school? What is it I'm supposed to do? What do these butterflies mean? What are you trying to tell me?"

Just then I remembered what I had said and promised upon two occasions: once was when I was in the midst of an intense fever during my cancer treatment and passing from this life. I was bargaining with God and pleaded with him as we all often do when faced with death.

"If you save my life I will become a fisher of men for you. I will fight for wounded souls, broken hearts, and anyone lost to give them HOPE."

The second time was when I gained my freedom and stepped out of the cancer clinic...my first battle had been won!

"God thank you for healing me. To show my gratitude to you for saving my life, I will become a fisher of men."

This is something my Nana had spoken to me about many times, to be grateful to something greater than ourselves. She would remind me, "It's not an instrument of execution that hangs from a gold chain around my neck – it's a symbol of God's love and sacrifice for humanity." (We used this line in one of our scripts in 1998) She wanted me to be humble and to always be respectful and give thanks to those that deserved it. However, it would quickly be forgotten by me and instead I responded in trepidation.

"Please just let me be, I'm too broken to do anything for anyone. I am of no use and no good to anyone in this condition. Plus this woman doesn't need me, she's fine and I'm fine and that's that."

...or so I coerced myself into believing. My attempts convincing God into siding with me and seeing things my way wasn't going to work. This would become apparent later on.

The fall months were still bringing the hot weather however the dance studio felt colder than it usually did, the floor reminded me of ice. I looked around and felt a dark presence. To this day I do not know what it was, but it was not good. I appreciated being able to work on this dance piece but I didn't feel secure in this space. Something about this entire place rattled my spirit, but this is where I was planted. These walls could probably share a million secrets but I didn't want to know any of them. I set the CD player on the floor, started the music and danced. Occasionally "The b-fly" would check in on me. I don't think she knew that I was I aware of her watching me at times. Not that I minded very much, but I could sense her presence and it gave me strength.

It also gave me joy to watch her dance in class. You could tell that she was a beautiful dancer when she was younger, not that her current age detracted from her skill, but I would say sorrow from the years weighed her down. My heart hurt for her in this respect, I wanted to do everything I could to bring some joy in her life to reciprocate the peace she hoped for in mine.

With every opportunity, I would help her, set the barres up in class, smile, say hello, and all the little things that can make a heart lighter. Unbeknownst to me, each little thing caused the thorn in my heart to burrow deeper and forced the light in my heart to grow and shine outwardly to her and others. Unnerving as it was, I just let it settle inside never imagining that it would continue to flourish and least of all hurt. Every once in a while it would hurt so much that I had to rub it and press against it with the ball of my palm. I did this when the MVP (mitral valve prolapse) would act up as well; a strange connection.

As requested by "The b-fly" to get a doctor's clearance note, on November 30, 2007, we were in Vegas to visit my cardiologist. He was a well-respected specialist and helpful with my situation. After the Doppler, EKG, ultrasound and other exams, he concluded what we already knew since my first diagnosis in 1993 under another specialist: I had an advanced stage of mitral valve prolapse. It had gotten worse since it was first detected, but there wasn't much I could do. The only reason I was there was to appease "The b-fly"; the dancing was helping this condition not exacerbating it.

To this day I still am perplexed why she had an issue with this and why she was so adamant about my seeking a physical clearance note. (I found out later from the school and also as my husband pursued a new career in law, that this is not legal to ask anyone for this information.) I tend to think that perhaps she had prior students who lied to her prolifically about their medical conditions to gain favor/attention or used as an excuse so they could give less than full 100 percent effort in class...or something. Perhaps she truly was concerned for me and didn't want me to pass out and die in her class; not that that was ever likely.

Nonetheless I was, not doing either: attention seeking or trying to gain favor. I was a full grown woman, nowhere near my teens or twenties with a husband and son. Attention seeking in a community college class wasn't even in my thoughts when I had already been on beautiful, professional, performance stages. Most of the time, I felt like the character Peggy Sue in "Peggy Sue Got Married" in which the character goes back to her high school days in the 1950s and relives it all as an adult.

This oddity my instructor had with my health was one that I had to let go of and put on the shelf for a time to remain unanswered. Ten years later I still don't know what her issue was.

After the heart exams, and paying a down payment on my medical bill which was over a thousand dollars, I went to see my Nana at the adult care home. I was very nervous about seeing her, what she would look like, the weight loss effecting her beauty and vitality, and how I would respond troubled me. Her cancer had returned for a second time and save for my speaking to her on the phone, I hadn't seen her for almost two years.

My husband, son and I stepped out of our SUV, and took a deep breath. My husband squeezed my hand, which still is a quiet gesture that secretly reminds me: "Breathe. You got this."

We knocked on the door and a sweet Mexican lady welcomed us. Food and beverages were offered to us immediately and there was Nana sitting perched on the couch with enormous bright eyes behind her large eyeglasses. This made me chuckle because she adored large rimmed eyewear that made her look like a spunky librarian from the 1980s. She had lost a lot of weight but it didn't detract. Age does not detract from the beauty of a rose. Nana was a rose. All the ladies in my family were small framed, petite beauties.

Our son and I dove into her arms as my husband looked on. He was ushered to another couch and was followed by a plate of food. Something in common with the Italians, which my family is, and Mexicans, they love to show hospitality and serve food galore. We loved these people who were taking good care of Nana.

I told Nana that I was dancing again and how hard I was working. She loved to hear all of this as we reminisced about our backyard in New Jersey. She was thrilled to hear how her grandson was succeeding in school, her little potata (she never said potato) was now a young teen. We were all doing fairly well.

I wanted very much to share with Nana that I had undergone treatment for my cancer but I didn't want to worry her or drag her down. She needed all the strength and good vibes she could get. Plus I was relatively fine for the moment. I was ALIVE and dancing again. She never knew that I was diagnosed with the disease while I was taking her for her radiation treatments in Las Vegas before we sold our home.

Nana knew we had to leave and get back to L.A. She gave me a wonderful hug and kiss. "Live. Live well and listen to your teacher. Bye angel." Angel was my special name that she often called me. She said it with strength and love. Her eyes looked at me as if it would be the last time I would see her.

CHAPTER 4
BEAUTIFUL STRANGER

"Compromise is an art form in which both parties need to care about the other one enough to see the other just as important as themselves."

It haunts & taunts, it enchants & flaunts. Some days it's blue, yellow, white; with tattered wings it delights taking flight...Breathe

Breaking transgression's waves, hearts, and sanity but along the way it forgot to...Breathe

Alas a mystery that has a conclusion that leads its followers through tumultuous calcified pulp it stopped breathing. This was its choice. Noelle Andressen

Summer 2012

December of 2007, was a trying time for me and my family. We had little money and could barely afford food. Many nights I went hungry just to be able to feed our son. This caused my body to weaken somewhat and for a dancer and a cancer patient, it is detrimental. Nutrition is vital. It was also at this time I had been presented with the opportunity to perform in an informal showcase.

Our class was told that anyone could perform since it was a casual class performance. It was under the direction of this beautiful stranger/"The b-fly" that I often spoke of. I was and am a hard worker and will always be one. I practiced this dance for hours every day but the damage in my body and memory was something I couldn't overcome at this time.

The daunting fear of performing in front of people was a huge issue for me, but I wanted to do this. I had to break the bondage of fear NOW. I had to live in complete freedom which to me is the absence of all fear and the fruition of HOPE. I knew myself well enough that if I didn't succeed now, I would never allow myself this chance again and would have given up forever.

The old saying: "Failure is not an option." held true for me. My Nana would say "Failure may not be an option, but it can be an opportunity." While her words were always wise, I was not going to accept failure at this time even if it turned out to be just a learning experience for me. Knowing that "The b-fly" believed in me helped a lot and kept me focused. She was and always will be a very fundamental person in my growth, with both positive and challenging aspects to it. It's complicated but triumphant.

This performance even though it was on a very small scale inside a dance studio, it became my world and fulfilled my second short term goal. I hadn't performed in years. I knew I could do this if I set my mind to it and had "The b-fly's" support. I didn't care that it wasn't on the grand Bob Hope McCallum stage where I met my college sweetheart and future husband. I only cared about two things: not letting "The b-fly" down again, and not failing myself.

The evening of December 6th, 2007, our class practiced her choreography. I loved the music, I loved the choreography, and I started to have a deep fondness for her. Normally, I would have chastised myself for having any type of feelings for anyone, but for some reason I let her in further. She had helped me thus far, I felt I could trust her. So I did.

When we began to rehearse the dance I realized that I was getting so confused and so lost in the movement that I couldn't do it perfectly and made mistakes. I told "The b-fly" that I was having a bad day. The pressure I had put upon myself was excruciating but I needed to nail this.

I condemned myself harder than a murderer before a jury. I had failed. "The b-fly" did not seem pleased with me at all and I felt that I had let her down once more. At that point she seemed to disown me and speak with the other ladies and younger girls in the class and I was pushed to the side. She said that I couldn't perform because I didn't know the piece well. Had I understood this correctly? She had just said that anyone could perform even if they made mistakes; so which was it?

She seemed to then dote on the others, praise them, and place them in position for the performance. I could have sworn that she sent a look of contempt my way in the midst of that. I failed her and she was making it known to me. I questioned if I perceived this correctly. She wasn't always easy to read and had an old school approach to ballet coupled with an odd form of "tough love". Not that I criticized her methods but it's not a manner that I employed or used to teach my students. I wondered if she had placed a higher level of expectation on me than I was able to deliver at that time. It was possible that she truly had projected and saw me as sort of a "favorite" in class and when I didn't perform perfectly this was her way of disciplining. This was not uncommon in the world of ballet. Praises often are given when perfection achieved and sullen glares of disappointment when anything less was attained.

That was it. I was finished. My silly idea of trying to dance again was over—time to quit. I walked away from the group and wondered if I had interpreted what had happened correctly. I wondered also if I should and could approach her to change her mind and to let me perform. Maybe she would help me I thought. She said when I first met her that she would help me fight. Other students verified that for me. Contrariwise, I had received my answer in her attitude towards me. She would not look at me for the remainder of the class. She was turning away from me like everyone else had in the past. A twinge of my past history being sexually abused as a child came forward and I intentionally took off those tainted lenses and chose to see things with a different perspective.

I slipped off my ballet shoes and held them in my hands for a moment as I watched her feet glide across the floor. She was still assisting and demonstrating for other students, she truly was a great dancer still, how much more incredible was she when she was younger I thought. Was she able to achieve everything she desired in life—in dance? Did she receive all the encouragement she needed to reach her full potential or was she criticized to the point that all dreams were hidden beneath layers of false shame and cynicism? My heart then broke for her.

Instead of focusing on how disappointed and hurt I was, I wanted to understand her position more. I wondered, could she have been treated this way too if she wasn't perfect? Wow she was taught and shown love? If it was, it's highly possible and probable it was wrong and abusive. No matter the background, I chose to behave responsibly and contemplate further what I could do if anything.

Many hours later in my home, it was 5:30 AM on the 7th to be precise, I placed myself in my most favorite spot in the world: the floor. The floor is either a dancer's faithful lover offering undying support or comfort but can also betray, deeply wounding if the connection and "marriage" wasn't consummated.

On my back, I could feel my breathing connect to the weight of gravity. I still could not believe that I had not done well enough in a college class to be able to perform. I had performed before in gorgeous venues and I had been a very good dancer. I kept a lot of this secret because I wanted to leave my past behind me and I also didn't want to seem prideful and brag. I didn't know what I had lost so much of that I was doing this poorly. Maybe I was doing well enough and there were underlying issues "The b-fly" had with me that were for her to own and not me. What troubled me most was that she seemed to disown me when she had been helping.

That hit the hardest and hurt the most.

After the torrent of confusion subsided, I watched shadows on our living room walls from the trees blowing in the wind. They looked like dancing sprites. With child-like joy I got up, curtseyed in my nightgown and danced with them. It was then that I had been inspired for my next dance. Shadow dancing. It later became known as "Fileo-Eros". I fantasized what the dance would be and played around with various pieces of music in the middle of the night. I didn't sleep.

The wall shadows kept dancing but I stopped. I traced my hand along their outlines. They looked so free and at peace…yes, peace, just like "The b-fly" said to me, she hoped I would find peace. I then decided to email her and see if I could change her mind or perhaps I had misunderstood everything.

Our seemingly breeched relationship didn't make any sense to me and I wanted to mend it. That too was another motive of mine as relationships are most important to me. While I was not a people pleaser, I loved people, but would be willing to compromise. Compromise is an art form in which both parties need to care about the other one enough to see the other just as important as themselves. If I was going to reach out, I had to do it because I wanted to achieve this for myself and have no other motive. It wouldn't be to win her over or gain her acceptance. I had to do this for me.

DANCE WARRIOR - FROM CANCER TO DANCER

"Fri 12/7/2007 7:59 AM - not knowing what to say

What I'm going to say is honest; I ask for your patience and graciousness as I try to explain and if there's a misunderstanding, then I ask forgiveness.

First, I think you're great and I trust you. Nothing changes that. My hardened heart, afraid to trust/love again because so many said they would help me only to turn their backs when I needed them, has softened. The fact that I can trust/love is miraculous. My heart made progress before the root of bitterness crept in. I plan to walk the rest of my days in love.

The first day of class when I told you my about my health I said I'd have to fight harder than others. You said you'd help me fight. No one has ever said that. I was overwhelmed. I saw something extraordinary in you; a quality few people have. I also could figuratively hear shackles being unlocked. Something that unjustly bound me for years was broken. I knew I was in the right place. I knew taking the first step, although it scared me, was right. Not only was dance brought back into my life but trust and something else that's beautiful that I can't articulate at this point.

Next step: the midterm dance combination. Not just do it, but do it well. Remember how frustrated I was, I wrote you how I couldn't figure out the dance combination, and then it all came together. I did more than pull it off, I danced well.

Next step: to finish well. Meaning: challenge myself to go where I feared—to not be afraid to perform again. I shared that illness took away a lot from me like confidence and I was left with tremendous fear—I don't like being in front of people let alone sharing my talents. All the years and practice being in front of people sharing my talents singing dancing writing trusting loving-all would be in vain when illness would rip away all that I was. Then cancer broke me--broke my heart. On the other side of it, I barely had enough fight left in my heart to take back what was stolen from me. Like a smoldering wick that still had a flicker of hope if just the right gentle breeze would blow and light it again. "I will help you fight" was that gentle breeze along with dancing.

But I'm hurting so deeply right now and I'm not always the world's greatest communicator so I'll explain what's inside: I want to quit, never dance again and hide, and yet I also want to fight harder, but I cannot without help.

I've never quit anything in my life. But two things are tempting me to quit: First-I feel that you don't believe in me to do well enough to get it together for Tuesday; then how can I believe in myself? I know you said if I tested well then performing is fine.

I feel that you don't believe in me to do well enough to get it together for Tuesday; then how can I believe in myself? I know you said if I tested well then performing is fine. But I thought this past Tuesday when I showed you my skirt and you said it was fine and then you asked in class who wanted to perform, I said I do, I assumed this meant I was going to perform because you didn't say anything otherwise, but I don't know. Tonight I didn't dance as well and I'm confused. I didn't understand why you were asking who was performing again tonight…maybe I missed something along the way…I don't hear well so that's very likely.

Please understand, I know you weren't trying to do anything to make me feel this way, I don't hold you responsible. But more importantly getting back to the essence of the point, I need you to help me fight as you once said you would because I'm losing big time and the smoldering wick barely exists. If I can't perform, it's ok, but what would break my heart, if this is true, is saying you'd help me fight then not. Those are such strong words and I've asked for little help and I've done all that you've asked of me. Before I took this class I got referrals and everyone said the same thing: you're a helper and care. As I said I'm very particular whom I spend my time with and I don't have any regrets but I need help.

I guess what I felt and translated in my head then in my heart was that you weren't going to help me fight and that you don't have faith in me. Is this true or am I a total dork and getting upset for no reason? I decided after bawling my head off, no sleep and giving myself a migraine that I should probably just be honest and ask you. Noelle"

I hesitated to hit "send". Knowing that if she took this the wrong way, this could potentially is the permanent dissolution of our budding relationship. I didn't know her well enough but others did. They gave me warning that she could behave oddly at times and be moody and switch things around. I cared too much to let this go. I had to know, I had to figure out a way to fix things if they were indeed torn and if I had done something that troubled her. She responded fairly quickly as usual and appreciated my honesty. Again, with respect to her, I will summarize her words.

She expressed that she was happy to help her students, and that there had been a miscommunication between us. She didn't recall stating that she would help me fight, however, several students heard her say this to me. She also stated that I had called her many times when there were no phone calls between us, I didn't even know her number. She said that there were also many emails but in counting only 5 email exchanges occurred between us. She also mentioned the many office visits, and I only met her in her office twice for a few minutes because she wanted to talk to me about my heart valve. She made it sound like she spent a tremendous amount of time with me. She hadn't. I was very careful of this because of how I was wounded in the past by being set-up this way. I've learned how to protect myself from these false attempts at relationships.

Confusion compiled as I further read her reply. It seemed like a mixture of a backpedaling attempt and also a hand reaching out to help me. I wasn't calling her out on anything, I earnestly wanted to know what was occurring, and if there was something I could do to change her mind and repair any relational damage between us. While I was perplexed at the apparent guilt-trip and inaccuracies, I was also relieved. It seemed that nothing was shattered and she was fine with all things concerning my performing and our relationship. She concluded that I could perform and was gracious about it. She had changed her mind. I shook my head perplexed and chalked it up to miscommunication and my over thinking things; but I would keep this in my memory and journal about it. A residue of *something* was very unsettling about all of this. This was why I didn't want to let anyone in as a similar instance happened to me once before.

Regardless of that, I was determined to finish what I started. It is the small things that amount to universal changes and puts forth a remedy to sway things old and new. Without these elements that compound and accumulate, our truths may never be found and yet somehow they find us if we falter on our quest. The universe beckons us to delve into the vastness of the universal truths and explore.

The night of the performance I giggled a bit while I was in my bathroom getting dressed. It was reminiscent of when I was a teenager in front of a makeup vanity. Hair pins, brushes, false eyelashes and underwear were strewn about every inch even on the floor. My husband bought a black leotard for me. It became the most precious thing to me because I hadn't had one in a very long time.

Upon my diagnosis, I had thrown out all my dance attire, dance photos, dance shoes, anything that had reminded me of what I lost. I just couldn't be around it while I was ill. The thoughts would be too tortuous and my heart ached deeply to not be able to dance. However, this night, I would take back everything that I lost. That was why it was so important for me to dance, I hoped I had conveyed this to "The b-fly". With one short 5 minute dance, I was about to conquer all that evil tried to kill within me and I felt like I had a portion of my question answered: I had survived cancer, for what purpose was I spared?

This night I would be reaching into what is unknown and making it known; finding the depths within and expressing it outwardly. At times like this we must stop to think about what and why we are doing the things we do. What is their cause and effect in this world?

Dancing in this performance did more than I anticipated as the many years ahead would prove to me. It had implications that went beyond my comprehension at the time. There was something else that needed to be done besides perform. I was giving a witness of my character to "The b-fly" who was drawn to me as much as I was to her, both of us not knowing why. I wanted to show my appreciation for her as did the other students.

My Nana had taught me proper etiquette and I wanted to give her the perfect gift. Then it dawned on me, a black and white photo of some of her students dressed in their costumes for the performance would be classy and appropriate. There were only four of us available so we did our best and posed. Our positioning was not a perfect *sur le cous de pied*, but it would have to do, we had little time. I rushed to the photo shop and they had a beautiful print done in minutes. I bought a frame and there it was—the perfect gift from the heart.

All of her students signed the back of it. I vaguely remembered what I wrote, "Remember how much you are loved." At that time I had no idea why I wrote that. Currently, I have some guesses but I may not find out for certain until years from now.

There I was, walking up the steps to the dance studio. My husband was on my right arm and my left hand was clawing at my tights. I was very nervous. "Take me home, this is a mistake. I'm gonna screw up and she'll be mad at me again."

"No, no. You've worked this hard and come this far. You've conquered cancer. I'm not taking you home. You are going to dance." My husband then reminded me of what he said to me in the cancer clinic when I had thought I was dying:

"You will rise from your sick bed. You have much yet to do. Breathe….breathe….breathe…" He helped me breathe through a tough hurdle then and now. "You've done harder things." He said and smiled knowingly at me.

He was right. I was going to do this little 5 minute dance for him, for our son, for "The b-fly", and definitely for me.

The few friends I had made in class were there and they were all supportive and loving. They knew of my battle and wanted me to succeed. We all gathered in the hallway and prepared to perform for our close friends and family in this intimate setting.

The studio went dark and we took our places at the barre. Our instructor choreographed a sweet dance. She had placed me towards the back which was a merciful act. If I messed up no one would see it. I remembered my husband telling me to breathe, so I did. With that first breath and first beat of music I was performing again. The music had a Celtic feel to it, one of my favorite types of sounds to dance to. I got lost in it and smiled, and enjoyed each movement. One minor mistake but I just kept on moving until it was over….and sooner than I wanted it to be, it was over. The lights went out, and the applause was appreciative. I secretly did a bow in the dark, it was like years ago on stage, and then I dashed out of that dance studio. I had dropped to my knees and kissed the floor. I had done it! I had done it well!

Within those precious five minutes, it felt like the flood gates of evil was banished to oblivion. With that proud moment I extended my middle finger to cancer. I whispered, "I got you."

"The b-fly" passed in front of me, "Are you okay?" I smiled and nodded my head. She didn't forget about my struggle and she cared. Perhaps I had read her intentions incorrectly all along. Yes, I would put our small incident on the back-burner and move forward. We gave her the picture framed photo gift and all seemed well. I think she deeply loved it.

Task one accomplished! One more task at hand. The most important one left: to dance for my husband.

The last night of class, after everyone went home I was given the dance studio to share a precious gift with my husband. I didn't think I could surpass the nervousness that I had for my first performance, but I did. My knees quaked and the thought "The b-fly" walking in while I was dancing for my husband would have compiled the angst exponentially.

My mouth breathed out my mantra, "You know what to do…breathe…breathe…breathe…" My eyelids felt heavy for a brief moment but then they sparked open. "I do know what to do." I confidently told myself.

With that, I started the music and danced to his favorite song, "Comfortably Numb" by Pink Floyd. The past 15 weeks led to this moment, a chance to salvage our marriage with dance. Since words had failed, I knew I was fighting for a way to pierce his heart with truth and light. I danced hard, I danced strong, I finished well.

With little breath in my lungs, I completed the last movement and collapsed to the floor. I brushed the hair from my face and saw his smile and I felt his love. It was like a gentle dove whispering its inviting song to its mate. I knew then that I had hit his heart hard. He was moved by my movement. I got up and touched my tender giant on his cheek, "I love you." No other words were said. No other words were needed. I had said it all with dance.

We drove home in a limousine which was both amazing and ridiculous since we lived across the street. On the ride home, I reflect back on my experience. It was important in many ways. It further imbedded a seed of love and HOPE in "The b-fly's" heart and mine. She showed that she did care and it was growing whether either of us wanted it to or not. I also did what I set out to do and danced very well. This was the best shortest drive down the street from the college to our front door.

We had a very special and intimate evening as we lay on our bed and drifted into slumber. It was the beginning of mending a lot of years filled with tears. In the middle of the half sleep state I felt a pinch in my right breast. I felt the area below my nipple, it was a small, hard lump near where the initial breast cancer location was found two years ago in 2005. No. Not tonight, it would have to wait. Tonight I beat my enemy: cancer, I whispered to myself. And that was how I decided to end my year.

CHAPTER 5
AT THE SHORELINE

"Shackles – broken, Cage – open, my wings just a little rusty."

This life is but a fleeting glimpse, a small drop in the ocean. Reflect....choose wisely ....breathe the free air....for someday all of our lives will break at the shoreline....but ponder ~ who will you meet there. Noelle Andressen

Santa Monica in the summer 2010.

The New Year had begun and so did the new semester. I had returned under the tutelage of "The b-fly" who was presenting an informal dance production. I had missed her and was glad to see her again. She seemed genuinely glad to see me as well and greeted me with a huge smile, "Hi, Noelle!". I had hoped that our little rough spots from the previous semester would be in the past and released it to stay there.

During this production, I met a lovely but shy elderly lady named Carol. We became close friends over time as she wasn't easily won over. Her husband of over 30 years had just passed on and her heart was understandably vulnerable. She also became a member of my dance company years later.

"The b-fly" mentioned she was looking for dances for the show. I'm not sure why I felt determined to choreograph a dance for this production, but I inquired about it. She agreed to my dance. She loved my music choice which had a blend of Aramaic and Hebrew words sung to an ancient world score. The theme of friendship pressed heavy on my heart and became the thrust of my dance.

We continued where we left off with our relationship the previous semester, all seemed well. It was great to discover that we had so much in common and I truly began to like her. Many others warned me again to be careful and not get too close to her. At that time I couldn't figure out why, even with our prior relational hiccups. All relationships have challenges, this wasn't new. We actually worked together well, similar to a mentoring situation. I was once again enthralled by "The b-fly" in my life and I wanted to help her for helping me.

She was also very good at teaching modern so I was enrolled in that class as well as ballet. I tended to think that she was not so unlike me in that while I loved ballet, I also liked to rebel against its rigidity. Perhaps though, I had more of a rebel spirit as I didn't like to always put my hair up and point my toes, I had to dance freely without inhibition like Isadora Duncan and express myself like Martha Graham.

On her credenza this semester, I noticed her notebook with a transparent sleeve on the front cover. There was a beautiful black and white photo of a dancer. I was immediately engrossed and fell in love with the artistry. It was a Lois Greenfield photo of a dancer under stretchy fabric. I loved the way the dancer's body was captured on film in a still moment, suspended in the air and in time. It was extraordinary.

Lois's calendars were also hung in her office. The images were all beautiful and mind-boggling. How was this style photography achieved? I had of course seen Lois's trademark photography before early in my training days around the early 1990's, how could one not notice them. I just didn't know who the photographer was and too "into" my young adult self to research. As a mature adult however, I did the research and fell more in love with this amazing artist and greatly wanted to work with her someday. At that time, I had to settle for gazing at "The b-fly's" photos and calendars and dream.

While we were having one of our bi-weekly meetings preparing for the concert, "The b-fly" shared how one of her student's lost their grandfather in the middle of a past dance production and she had to leave for the funeral. She said she felt that she was pegged as the "bad guy" for having to drop this student from the show, but the student didn't know when she'd return and had to move forward with the production. I felt badly for her, I knew what it was like to have to make such a hard decision, but I also found it odd that this resonated deeply with me when she said this. I wasn't sure why so I put it in a "holding cell" in my heart for the moment.

She shared intimacies about her family and her schooling. She had it rough but I respected her for having gone through it all, it was not an easy life. Still I sensed there was more, a lot more beneath her smile.

With each of her stories, often I found myself defaulting to putting up my wall again; however, I felt obligated to reciprocate and shared a few things here and there. I've been down this cobblestone path of pain before. The shade from the emotional trees felt somewhat familiar but it was delivered from a different one's face, a different one's story. *It can be different this time.* I thought to myself but I was afraid to open a door because of past disappointments. I also knew that it could change and be better this time around but I didn't know if I had any more love inside of me to risk being broken. This precious woman was sharing her heart with me, at least I could listen and care and at least express some of my things on that level. I did share with her that my Nana said to listen to her and so I did…for the most part. I conveyed that my Nana wanted me to LIVE, and dance, and do all these wonderful things.

"The b-fly" showed a few photos to me, one in particular I loved. It had a beautiful woman underneath a shear piece of fabric. It was gorgeous and I was inspired. I told "The b-fly" I wanted to do a dance with fabric someday; and I did. It was called "The Silent Rose". I never saw her dance, only that one photo. I'm certain our dances were not similar. Four years later she would see that dance, but I never saw hers.

We had a lovely time every other week or so for a half hour in her office, chatting mostly about dance and the dance production and new ways that I could help her. In between all of that she shared some more stories and I finally started to open up and share too. I offered to do sewing, graphics, anything that would help. I had a lot of time open to do as we dreamed.

She emailed me how much she appreciated all that I was doing and was impressed that I had talents hiding everywhere. She thanked me for my dedication. I stopped a moment and thought: "Is she for real or is she playing me to smooth over what happened last semester? Like atonement?" Again, this was odd. I didn't think about my talents, I just knew to help people and so I replied to her.

Sunday 03/02/08 at 4:19 PM – (my reply)

Re: talents--in all honesty, most of it was birthed because I was sick. I didn't/don't take lying in bed "lying down"-lol. I guess now I can't keep it all for myself, I have to give. I've done a lot in my short life thus far, but I never really "lived" my life and now I feel like I'm coming alive. I hope this doesn't sound corny but you've inspired me to keep going.

Shackles-broken
Cage-open
my wings just a little rusty
See you Monday, Noelle

Weeks in that semester passed on and the sharp pinching in

my right breast soon turned into sharp stabbing pain. I don't know if during class, "The b-fly" or anyone ever saw me flinch or grab at what may have seemed to be my armpit, but I knew at some point soon I'd have to deal with it, but it wasn't going to be now.

Later that day, my aunt had called to let me know that Nana's cancer returned again. I couldn't manage any more stress. I kept the breast pain secret for a time longer as I didn't want to be a burden, especially to her.

In the next few days my best friend Sheila in Vegas was trying to figure out a way to fly me to see my Nana one last time. We all knew it was close to the end for her. Nothing we tried worked. Sheila texted me *"we gotta find a way to get you to see your Nana."* I knew she was right and her heart's motives pure, but I also felt that it wasn't meant to be. There was another plan for my life, another purpose at this time and I wouldn't be able to see Nana again.

St. Patrick's Day March 17, 2008 was unfolding in a beautiful way. I had finished my costumes for my dance piece and was excited to show them to "The b-fly" for approval. She was very particular about things and I didn't mind this aspect of it at all. For this Monday's appointment she said 1:30 pm would be good for her. We talked more about dance and the production and some beautiful personal things. I was really starting to let her in. Trust was being built.

As we chatted at our meeting my cell phone buzzed. I looked down at my purse where it was tucked away. I could tell by the alert that it was my brother. Only nights before I prayed that God wouldn't let my Nana suffer. I had a feeling what it was about. I didn't want to answer it. I knew that my Nana was gone and my brother was calling to let me know.

While my heart dropped out, I had a sense of peace. Then I felt a warm brush against my soul. It was Nana. I believed she was saying goodbye for now, but that she was pleased, well pleased with me and that she wasn't sad that I couldn't make it to Vegas to see her one last time. I felt her presence letting me know that I was exactly where I was supposed to be, with who I was supposed to be with. I didn't answer my phone because I already knew what had happened and could do nothing to change things. I wondered if my instructor questioned why I wouldn't pick up my phone, or if she noticed that it was signaling me. Additionally, I didn't like crying in front of people, and if I did I was allowing a special vulnerability that was a privilege.

We wrapped up our meeting and I walked home clutching my purse to my chest. My tears were held back by my fear of anyone seeing my distress. A white butterfly made a brief appearance and I gasped. Was this a sign that my Nana was okay? The white darling flew away. "Come back." I squeaked out. The dam of tears broke and I ran home.

I cried on my couch for an hour or maybe it was two. My sense of time had been warped and all things seemed surreal. As a dancer you rely on your feet to meet and find the floor, they had never failed to do that. This time I couldn't find the floor to comfort me. Nana was like a mom to me, substituting for my true mother most of the time. I had managed to speak with my brother. He confirmed it, Nana was gone. I always have had a sense of this type of thing, dammit I wished I was wrong.

I emailed "The b-fly" with a huge dawning upon me. She had just shared with me how a former student had something similar happen. I didn't want her to worry and I didn't want her to think I wasn't returning or that I would desert her like another student did. It's strange how with just a few words spoken we can be prepared for something in the future. Was she divinely used to foreshadow and prepare me for Nana's passing? It was very thought-provoking to me. I emailed that my Nana had died and she sent her blessings. Then I realized another thing: if it weren't for her demanding a doctor's clearance note, I would not have seen Nana one last time before she died.

My aunt and I discussed services for Nana. We decided she should have a Christian service being that she was Catholic and then later in life chose a non-denominational Christian belief. My aunt asked if I still knew the pastor who renewed my and my husband's wedding vows. I said yes.

With that are some irony and some interesting heartstrings that were inadvertently plucked. This pastor and his wife were the leaders in the church that my family was wounded in. This too would deserve an entire book for itself. My journals contain the pain like a jar of tears. For now, we will leave it at that.

We arranged for this pastor and his wife to officiate the family service memorial for Nana the following Friday. They knew her, and knew my family. They agreed and I was actually looking forward to seeing them after not seeing them for many years. I chuckled at the intricacies of life.

It had been a long time ago since this wound occurred. I was already healing from that chapter of my life by letting "The b-fly" into my heart. These things seem to present themselves again in life, to test us. I was about to see if I could pass this test: bittersweet or bitterness. I was: Healing my past so that I could have a future. This would be a good thing.

The following night I went to class. I didn't want to be alone in my sorrow. I wanted to be among the living, dancing, and this is what I did. I stayed in the back of the room by myself, by my own choice. For now, we will also leave this at that. I went home after class and wrote in my journal:

If I could imagine the most incredible day...it would begin with rising in a completely healthy body with no remembrance of the horrors of the past. A stroll on the beach and the brisk ocean waves chasing my feet as the white foam crests along the shore. I wouldn't be alone. On either side of me would be my 2 greatest loves.

One my soul-mate and lover the other my deepest love who's spirit has enraptured my heart since his birth. It would be ever so sweet for the 3 of us to etch our love for one another in the sand. We would marvel at this mighty creation, vastness and unmeasurable weight of love. We would form beautiful music with our heartstrings and reflect on our time spent together knowing that our lives are like the waves, one following the other with perchance to meet the shore at the same time.

Just as the sea foam breaks on the shoreline, so does man's life on earth. Each wave; each life; temporary and fleeting. Each serving its own purpose.

Nana's life and mine crossed for a time, her wave led and mine follows. Hers broke at the shoreline while mine continues for a time. I know God met her there at the shoreline…she was not broken any more.

Nana was not broken any more. She would not be tormented by the horrors of her life and freed from the pain of the past. Illness would not reach her, youth and beauty never leaving. Her body would no longer get tired and she would be dancing like the majestic queen she was. I felt more peace wash over me like soothing waves on the shore. I would miss her greatly.

The next day I informed "The b-fly" I wouldn't be missing any classes and that I was returning. I stressed this so she should would not worry or panic that I wouldn't return. She wished me well and said to take all the time needed to gather myself afterward. No classes were missed and I met all my deadlines and commitments without failure.

We found ourselves again in Vegas. Las Vegas, we escaped this place to seek healing for my body. Healing was found but at a high price. I never wanted to come back to the land of my suffering, however, there I was. There we all were again.

We parked in front of the wellness home that Nana lived in. Our former pastor and his wife drove up a few moments after our arrival. My husband clasped my hand, "Breathe…" I laughed, this word had a new meaning to it now.

We got out of our vehicle, it seemed like being at the top of a roller coaster hill. Once the car peeks at the summit, gravity takes over and there's nothing you can do to stop it. So I did what I do on rollercoasters: I put up my arms and enjoyed the ride. I embraced my former pastor's wife. The love was still there and any fault or blame I had towards her melted away. It is amazing what love can do. Not that we just allow abusive things to happen to us, but we can certainly learn to forgive and move forward.

She called me sweetheart and held me in her bosom. She expressed how sorry she was for my loss and walked into the home together. This may sound cliché but it was as if nothing ever happened and with that embrace torn chords were re-tethered together.

Inside, my entire family was there, brothers, aunt, mom and her boyfriend, uncle, Nana's caretakers, and the other ladies and gentlemen that lived there.

I hugged my mom. I hadn't seen her in years. There was an emotion in her eyes, a knowing of something that was separate from Nana's passing, "What is it, mom?"

She shook it off, "It's nothing. We'll talk another time. It's good to see you. You look good."

I had no idea what it was. I squeezed her again.

Over her shoulder on the counter was a gorgeous photo of Nana, and alongside of it, her ashes in a box. A box. That was Nana they told me. It was not her. She was a larger than life woman, vibrant, loving, hysterical, and beautiful. She was not a box of ashen memories to be stored on a closet shelf. I walked up to it and looked at it for a few seconds then sat down. That was not Nana.

I have been spared seeing any of my family member's lifeless bodies. I have seen a few corpses strewn on roads with sheets covering most of their remains and also at the morgue in Vegas when we were shooting our docu-drama "Baby Doe's Heartbeat". At a distance, I've seen at Wiefels Mortuary a dead, unknown, woman lying in a coffin. We were forced to go to this mortuary for a college class when I was 16.

I do not want to see anyone's lifeless body. I cannot handle this. If I were to see this up close, I would break. I could see myself attempting to resuscitate the person. Death rattles my inner being and shatters my core. I had a hard enough time when our pet praying mantis died. We were meant to live. I firmly believe that while death is a reality, it was never supposed to be this way, spiritually speaking.

While the pastor spoke beautiful words, my uncle who sat next to me bawled his eyes out and I grieved with him. We held each other. What else could we do? This woman meant a lot to many people and she would be missed.

This was the second, most grueling day of my life. The ultimate worst day would present itself only four and a half years later.

For you and your experience, it will happen in only a few chapters from now. Interesting, what took a few years in time, is reduced to only a few moments, a turning of a few pages. It's like looking on a cell phone calendar. You can quickly flip through the years in seconds, but to live it takes a life time.

After the tissue box was passed around the room and the ceremony completed, I said goodbye to our old pastor and his wife. I reflected on the past, how she was my spiritual mother at one time. I hugged her goodbye and we both smiled. I haven't seen her since. Occasionally, I would receive an email from her. While this relationship has mended somewhat, this particular story is far from over. I have this sense that I'll be visiting her someday.

My aunt had gathered all of Nana's things and split them up among the grandchildren and the rest of the family. She had so many photos, mementos, papers, and trinkets. We had a good time remembering her life and laughing about all the "Lucy Moments" that seemed to just "happen" to her. Not a perfect woman, but she loved her family and she loved God most of all.

Nana's death brought a reunion for my family and a healing with my past relationship that was severed between my pastor's wife and me. It was a beginning that I never believed would happen but hoped for.

It was time for goodbye. We had a life in L.A. and responsibilities that we couldn't disregard. I said goodbye to my family and I looked at my mom wondering what she wanted to tell me. I told her I was dancing again. She raised her eyebrows and gave her vague approval with her cute hippie-pixie smile. I don't think she grasped what I was telling her but she was thrilled for me. For the first time I think my mom actually approved of my dancing. There wasn't a butting of heads at all. This was the best compliment I received.

She said to come visit her on her boat in Florida. She was living her dream and made it happen. I knew mom well enough to know that there was more she wanted to say to me but didn't. My words of wisdom to you the reader: Don't hesitate to say things because you just never know. There are some things that are certain and there are some things that are unknown. You must seize every moment you have because you don't know if you'll have those moments again.

On our drive back to Los Angeles the vibration of the wheels on the road lulled me to sleep. In my dreams Nana visited me and told me to get my breast checked. I did. It didn't take long to get the news. My nemesis had returned for a second battle. The warrior within me rose up. I was furious.

CHAPTER 6
LIFE BEGINS WHERE FEAR ENDS

"I dance my scars to show that you too can heal."

Though the oceans of long suffering are stormy, you sail on a ship of faith and your harbor is peace. Noelle Andressen

© Jared Kale 2014

Many people live with and battle cancer for years. A breast cancer battle can sometimes last 12-15 years with intermittent lapses of remission. This can be seen in various cancers. It seemed that my road would be forever plagued with this disease, making an appearance whenever it wanted. My Nana had already died from it, I came close to succumbing to it as well. I did not want this as my legacy. I was just beginning to live, I didn't want to die.

My men folk at home were supportive and ready to jump into action. However, I decided to stave off treatment until after the show. I wasn't sure which treatment I would use, the one prior or try a new method. In the past I used a combination of clinical traditional treatments, with some medications and naturopathic means to treat the disease. It wasn't easy and I was very ill. It doesn't seem to matter which route you choose. You are going to feel horrid. You are fighting for your life. The path you choose to save it doesn't matter. Do whatever it takes to save your life. Choose something that you feel good about, can afford, and get support for. Every time I had to choose, I had to consider these elements. My choice will differ from yours. I always say: "My body – My choice."

I was mostly angry when I got the news. I didn't want to go through this again. It was hideous the first time. I also wanted to finish the dance concert, which too was my choice. How do I tell "The b-fly"? Do I tell her?

I was pressured to inform her by the other students so she wouldn't worry but if she didn't know, there would be nothing to worry about. They offered to tell her for me. I decided no, I'll do it, best it come from me than from them. They were at least 10-15 years my junior, and while I loved them, who knows how and what they would say. I really didn't want to tell her but they were probably right, it was the responsible thing to do in case she saw me not feeling well.

Nervously I said to her, "They found a lump. I don't think I can do this again. I don't want to talk about it."

She told me that she would then have the right to tell me whether or not I could continue choreographing/dancing. I said, "No, don't do that to me, that will kill me. I really don't want to talk about it." I didn't mean for the definition of my words to sound so grave, but I knew I had to keep going and keep fighting. If I quit cancer would win. I wasn't going to end up in bed like last time. She wanted me to take baby steps. I didn't have time for baby steps. Didn't she know that cancer could claim my life at any moment. Cancer takes people quickly. My entire life was lived carefully, I was not going to live cowering before cancer any more. I was choosing to live my dreams fast and hard.

I wanted to carry on with dancing. I knew I could dance through this if I had the support. I'm uncertain what she thought, but I wasn't asking her or pressuring her to help me, I was informing her of my situation so she wouldn't worry. However, even though I trusted her, looking back this was a huge mistake. I should've kept it to myself completely.

Since my husband and I decided to postpone the actual treatment for a short time, we decided to strengthen my immune system first and do various cleanses and the things I knew to do. The days were filled with struggle as my body was being prepared to receive another round of various treatments. It was already proving to be challenging and waking up in the morning a seemingly impossible task. Most of my doctors were in another country which demanded careful coordination and planning. I was angry I had to do this again.

Convicted of a crime just for being alive; this is how I felt. I couldn't believe that I found myself here again repeating steps from the past. Familiarity caused some of it to be easier with this reprise. My journal became filled with anger and frustration.

Why this again? What did I do wrong? I was just making strides in my rehabilitation. In the arc of my life, every time I began to get up and succeed at dancing, something pushed me down. I questioned God and am now embarrassed to admit that I had hate towards Him. I decided that I would not allow myself to end up in bed. If He wasn't going to help me then I'd do it all on my own in my own strength with or without other's help. I did not care. I was not going to falter at the hand of this ruthless disease.

I kept dancing. Some days were worse than others where my body ached and was so stiff I couldn't bend my fingers. My kidneys weren't handling the influx of medications and supplements. I had rashes on my stomach and chest. This reaction burdened my heart valve as well. I tried to hide symptoms from "The b-fly", but her sense of intuition and inquisitiveness was not easy to persuade otherwise. She would know if I was feeling well or not.

The last thing I wanted to do was burden her with my garbage. My heart was in the right place not wanting her to worry but she reacted intensely to my condition and it didn't always go over well.

These reactions caused a conflict between us and it grieved my heart. I told her I helped her because I cared and was taught to do the right thing by showing respect. She had some unspoken issue with my deep care for her and yelled at me. It seemed I had inadvertently "pushed her buttons" or innocently stumbled upon her sensitivities. Then again, she never shared with me about being sensitive to cancer or having issues with it, so I couldn't possibly be held responsible for button pushing. Intention does matter and my only intention was to inform and help. For the time I let it go.

The semester was almost over and the dance concert nearing. It was all coming to an end soon. My partner and I attended an annual consortium with some of our fellow students. It included all the colleges in the L.A. area in which students would perform their pieces. It was a great expression of community and became a short term goal of mine to present work in this venue in the future.

It was there I fell in love with a dance program from another college in Ventura. I met two of my future mentors who are now the greatest friends and colleagues of mine. I inquired about their program, found out they had an AA degree for dance (which I did not have, but I had a BFA), and put myself under their wings for the next 2 years starting that summer in which I was going to be fully immersed in my treatment. I chuckled at my ambition and positive thinking, however I had nothing to lose.

My partner and I performed at our concert and it went well.

Days after the concert was performed, I had received preliminary test results. It was not good. It showed that the cancer was spreading. I hoped there had been a mistake.

I said goodbye to two of my instructors. "The b-fly" told me to remember what my Nana had told me. I had forgotten myself then recalled Nana's words: "Live…" "The b-fly" was never one to openly share her emotions in public unless deeply moved. She knew how to conceal everything. Her communication was laced with hints and innuendos of compassion but then there were the past conflicts. It took me years to figure out this puzzle of apparent ambiguity. I knew that underneath the stone wall there was a flesh heart that desired to be understood. Not so unlike me. Maybe someday I would share with her that I understood, but it wasn't at this moment. We said goodbye for the summer months.

I thought a lot about my Nana over the summer and how I missed her dearly. I would write journal entries and childishly hoped that somehow she could sit alongside of me and read what I wrote:

<u>*~ If i could talk with you ~ one last time ~*</u>
I miss your precious Christmas kisses
I miss your sweet laughter
I miss your strength in god that you lived daily before my eyes
I miss your crazy antics
I miss your kindness
I miss your hugs that always made things better
I miss our prayer time together
I miss our late night movie watching
I miss our phone conversations

...and if I could talk with you one last time...
I would say: thank you that you never gave up on me, that you never gave up on praying for my soul to be saved, that you saw the beauty in me when I didn't, that you were never afraid to tell me the truth even when I didn't want to hear it, that you forgave me when I wasn't kind to you. Thank you that you showed me who god truly is ~ at least we had that time together...
~ I know that your spirit visited me on your way to heaven & you saw why I couldn't be with you ~ I had to stay behind to be with another soul to show the love of god ~ this is what you taught me to do ~ the way you showed the love of god to me ~
I love you nana ~ I do hope god lets you see me dancing.

Time, tests, and money would prove that while cancer had returned, and it had advanced, it was not as bad as it was first feared. A second and third battery of tests would bring conflicting results and minor consolation…the fight continued. I also continued with expanding my duet into an ensemble piece at this new college in Ventura. It was a great experience and I met many wonderful dancers who some currently dance in my company. I progressed with my rehab/treatment unbeknownst to them.

Some days were spent in the restroom vomiting, some days a little late for rehearsal, some days were a blur. I didn't make the same mistake again and I kept my pain and disease hidden from everyone. The treatment while challenging, it was kinder this time. My doctors knew how my body responded to the prior treatment and were able to keep me from being bed ridden. I had only two days that caused me to stay in bed. My mission more than accomplished.

Since my doctors adopted an Eastern philosophy and approach with medicine, they encouraged me to do yoga. I took a community class with a teacher I already was familiar with. She was very helpful and convinced this made the difference in my recovery.

The outside world didn't and wouldn't know about my health condition. I not only kept my disease private, but also that I was attending this new college; especially from "The b-fly". There was something inside of me that was cautious to not let her know the truth about this new college I was attending; for some reason I felt that she would take it as a betrayal although there was nothing I was betraying her with. We had this inexplicable connection and it was frayed. Since I treasured it, I wanted to proceed carefully and not do anything to cause it to tear permanently.

This new ensemble dance would be flawlessly performed and the photographs turned out gorgeous. I fell in love as I normally do, with a new dance family and they embraced me with all of my flaws and sensitivities. It was a lush campus and the air felt peaceful. I would make this my new home until I had attained the AA degree.

When I would least expect it, a butterfly would present itself to me and I would think of the beautiful stranger/"The b-fly" that started me on my path to recovery and essentially back to my professional dance career. My heart would ache knowing that things weren't perfect between us, and I couldn't figure out what went wrong, but again I had a greater hope that somehow, no matter how long it took, things would reconcile. For now, I would enjoy my artistic stay at this new place.

The fall season came quickly. I was staring at my cell phone waiting for it to ring. My doctors would have news for me. It rang and my heart palpitated. It was good news: remission again but the news would also state that a recurrence highly likely. I had to stay under close scrutiny and watch what I consumed, what I was around and keep my stress low.

While I was signed up for classes at both colleges, I wasn't sure if I'd attend both. It would mean taking over 11 classes a week combined. I had to choose, so I chose both and it may not have been the wisest decision, but I was compelled. I also wanted to tell "The b-fly" the good news or at least part of it. She would at least be happy for me. I was wrong, she was detached and uncaring. This didn't seem like her, there was something else behind all of this that had happened between us. I would find out more lately after several years and this too will not be mentioned in this particular writing but soon.

I was also compelled against my nature to create a dance about the child molestation I suffered for the annual fall showcase. It would not be lyrical or ballet. "The b-fly" had challenged me in the past to try something new. This was now. This was the time. This is where "Red Ribbons" began. Unbeknownst to me then, this would mark the beginning of my professional dance company and a return or continuation of my dance career. This would be a gift of love that would be presented as a message that stated I understood and an attempt to mend my relationship with "The b-fly".

NOTE: Most of this story will be fleshed out in my book "Dance Warrior - Red Ribbons Shattered Innocence". An excerpt is included at the end of this book. As we often find in time on earth that our life stories are multi-faceted and overlap with other's stories, they also overlap with several timelines in our own tales as subplots. This would be the case with "Red Ribbons". The depths of that cross over into my growth from cancer to dancer and played an important part in redefining me and my artwork.

Weeks trudged along with fatigue, frustration, and the fear that "The b-fly" would find out I was attending another college, were common elements in my undertaking for this season. I was continuously dealing with the cancer coming and going, the friction and rupture with two fragmented relationships: one with my husband and the other with "The b-fly", and then also completing my AA degree in dance caused great stress.

Ridiculous as it was for me to go backwards since I already had a BFA, I knew I had to humble myself and re-earn the discipline and lost technique to continue ahead. I didn't know what the path beyond that looked like, as I didn't know exactly where I was going except forward. I trusted in FAITH to light the way as needed and not one moment sooner.

Working on the "Red Ribbons" dance piece was painstaking. Doing it was not by free will but free choice to be obedient to what my heart was telling me to do. My dancers and I had just finished rehearsing and we were rushing to our dance classes.

I had my red folder with my choreographic notes and class assignments from the other college with me while at the original college campus. Accidentally, I left it in the hallway. Later, I had found it in an obscure place and the map of the other college was out and on top of it. My heart dropped. I had hoped "The b-fly" didn't see this. She would be more hurt at this point as things grew more complicated between us. I collected my folder and noticed that she was the only one besides me in the building. I put my hand to my head and left without her seeing me. I believed she saw my folder.

The day came for my dancers and I to show "The b-fly" "Red Ribbons" and present this gift for her to say thank you and that I understood. The dance, dancers, and I were impeccable. We knew we had done a great job, but things went incredibly wrong and completely opposite to what I planned. This story section too will remain for another time and another place. I will share that it did not go well. Between my not feeling well, her sensitivities, grand miscommunications, and my outspokenness, it was as the kids said, "a hot mess!" We exchanged passionate words, neither of us yelling but avidly meant. It was most likely fueled by an intensely performed dance and other factors that neither of us knew about the other. I could feel a "push-pull" yo-yo effect. We both wanted to be near one another but then again we both had our "wall issues" around our hearts to overcome.

My take on the situation from my end that I owned, is that while my words were right and accurate, my timing was incredibly wrong. I should have waited for a better time and place to speak and have since learned a valuable lesson that I would never repeat again. This is what repentance means: to change direction or one's ways.

It was only a week before our quartet of ladies would perform "Red Ribbons" for an audience. At this point she and I couldn't even look at one another when we passed in the hall or in class. Our heads hung down low. I had questions, she didn't want to give any answers.

The end result was that we could perform my piece but it was censored. At that time I thought it was her that did that, however, time proved to illuminate other facts to me. My heart was crushed that this wouldn't be performed in the way I intended it to be presented, I hoped the message wouldn't be lost.

The audience was silent and then erupted with great applause. My dancers and I were so proud. Movement spoke louder than words. It revealed the heart and reached the soul. We had just touched many. After the show, a woman came up to me and fell into my arms. She hugged me and said, "Thank you for saying what I couldn't." I knew with confidence that this woman had gone through something similar. I also knew that I reached her heart and helped her take the first step towards healing which also helped heal me too. I then thought maybe I should do this more often and dance stories; my stories—I dance my scars (the malevolent things I experienced) to show that you too can heal.

It's an oddity how even wickedness and darkness can betray itself and serve as an effervescent vessel to bring its own doings into the light by will or by force.

Then something familiar like an old friend resurfaced in my mind. My former pastor's wife would often tell me: "If you feel sorry for yourself, or feel depressed, reach out to others and help them." That was a key to healing for some people. It was for me and it was also how I could heal from my past so I could have a future. Have a corner of darkness in your life? Shine a light into it and watch a miracle transpire. Take what is negative and bad and turn it into good. Secrets and lies hide in darkness. Take those skeletons out of your closet and make them dance; and that is what I did.

The seed of my calling started to break through the fertile ground of my heart.

At the end of the evening I reflected at how far I had come in one full year. A lot had happened. I saw "The b-fly" at the stereo cabinet and I approached her. I wanted to cry, I wanted to say something that would change things.

I put my red ribbon that I had danced with in her hand and said, *"Thank you, I couldn't have done it without you."* I meant no facetious attitude in my statement. I was taking ground back over the evil that tried to divide us without placing blame on her. It was my way for attempting to do what I should have done to begin with. This was my gift.

I knew with certainty if I continued to pursue the relationship at the wrong time or prematurely, some things would be etched permanently on a tablet of irreparable damage. Some battlegrounds of the heart cannot be tread upon, and if one is brave enough to entertain the notion of exploration, one may not be prepared for what they may find.

A week later, she was sweet enough to write a precious note to me. I have it still. This note scared me and ultimately caused me to leave. I wanted to embrace her and mend everything, I think she also wanted that, but I couldn't. I was scared. That wall that she penetrated, the thorn of love that slipped in when we first met was blossoming. The intricacies involving our relationship are tender and I hold them dear to me, but I just couldn't keep this yo-yo relationship going.

The next semester at this new school would be more demanding and I couldn't attend both. I couldn't share that with her, I didn't want to hurt her or have her feel betrayed.

I gave her a hug goodbye and told her I wasn't coming back. This hurt deep but I knew I couldn't balance this demanding schedule and my fear was greater than my love at that point. I ran back into the hallway. She drove away.

My husband who traditionally picked me up after class, met me and comforted me. I showed him the note and what happened. He knew how much she meant to me. My wall had been broken down and collapsed that night. I had truly learned how to not only dance again but LOVE.

"It'll be okay. It'll work out in time." He consoled.

Work OUT?! How? It was over. I didn't think I'd see her again. Our relationship at that time had been severed due to circumstances beyond my control or knowledge at times. I loved her very much. I had to let her go. I had to trust in something greater than myself that she would be all right. Complete surrender was the strongest place to be in. It was when I laid down my worry and pride and picked up my humanity.

CHAPTER 7
RED RIBBONS

"It is important to remember that your feet know the way and will guide you in the midst of a storm."

There is a beauty that tells a tale of strength. Noelle Andressen

"Red Ribbons" Choreographed by Noelle Andressen 2008

I was given the opportunity to re-create "Red Ribbons" uncensored at this other college in which I was getting my AA in. I seized the moment and felt relieved that I could move forward and restore my artwork. A wonderful, sweet, woman mentored me through the process. She added an element of excitement to this piece.

Together we tweaked some things, added two sections including a short film, a tableau, and the end result was a piece I was completely happy with.

There was no drama, no manipulation games, no censorship, perfect peace. The experience was a dramatic opposite. It remains one of the best times in my history. I was warned that Moorpark was a conservative community and that my piece may rattle some hearts. My response: "GOOD!" That was the intention. If nobody talks about this subject matter, then no one will overcome this subject matter.

We choose to overcome or we choose to succumb. My warrior cry is Overcome! It must be. It had to be. This would become my dance company's mission. I was also setting the stage for those who would come after me to rattle hearts in their own ways.

At this point in time, it didn't matter what I made people feel as long as they felt something. That was my intent: to get the audience to feel something. If they felt nothing, then I failed—I didn't do my job correctly if this happened. All the gorgeous technique in the world wouldn't matter if I could not touch and reach precious and hurting hearts. I believed I had a remedy for their hurts.

On my half hour drive up the 118 highway, I'd practice my singing and think about happy thoughts. I had a challenging schedule with more than 15 hours a week dancing and choreographing. I thought, "What would a day be like with the absence of light, love, peace or…goodness? What if our lives were stripped of: poetry, beauty, art, music, dance…just for one day. What would remain: would be a sepulcher filled with skeletal remains called the ghost of humanity. I couldn't imagine this in our world however, I wanted to implement it into a dance and I would in 2013 and called it "the art of brokenness".

As I drove over 35 minutes, my breakfast beverage spilled over onto the console, the biscuits bounced on the passenger seat, and various dance shoes and attire was strewn all over the SUV. Not one of my tidy periods in my history; there would be time for cleaning afterwards, I just had to get through and reach my goal.

On the way up I'd also choreograph in my head and figure out what I needed to present to my dancers that day in choreography class or for my performance piece in the concert. Things would distract me as I'd pass through green hills. There was a large cross jetting out from on top of a hill peak. It left me wondering about my purpose in life. I questioned if I was doing what I was created to do; most of the time I was certain and then sometimes not.

One particular morning on my drive up the winding road to the campus, I was thinking about "The b-fly" and wondered how she was doing. A flock of orange butterflies flew overhead. It wasn't two or three, it was hundreds of them! It was an awesome sight. A massive movement of joyous color using their wings to rise above earth's troubles and migrate somewhere more suitable. I yearned to go with them. For now I had to remain deeply rooted into the ground like a rose and bloom at this other location. As for this day, I was headed in for hours of long rehearsal time.

She was gentle and sensitive to my needs and she comforted me during a trying process of healing from rejection and all that happened to me prior. She was aware that I was also dealing with another level of healing from the abuse in my past; I had thought I was done with the process but I wasn't. Often time we would chat in her office over a cup of tea. My body still got cold too easily so I would put the cup in between my hands to help warm myself. As our meetings progressed she gave me a larger and larger cup to drink from as she noticed how it was helping me. We often found ourselves discussing various and random things about life, dance, and theories, it gave me comfort to know that my art was important and that I was important too. Feedback on how to improve my technique and dance piece was always given in kindness she understood my ailments and helped me through them without judgment or harsh criticism. There were no games being played, no ostracizing or putting one student against another, it was a happy family with the typical mishaps occurring but nothing heart draining or hurtful.

The strange events that surrounded this dance at the other college caused me to look deeper inward and I found more brokenness. The depth of that brokenness found me on my knees at times; I felt betrayed from my past experience. She helped me work through all of it and was a great support. She showed me how to harness this and express it in my dancing. My voice mattered and she was determined to help me know and express this on stage, during rehearsals and in life.

We often had our "inner circle" with my dancers and would discuss how we were feeling during the rehearsal for this dance piece. So many young ones have been touched by abuse in such a detrimental way. There was a grave need for people to be able to talk about these things in a safe place. I kept this in the back of my mind as we progressed further as a strong team of women. This was a time of intimacy and we knew fate brought us all together.

While I was finishing up my degree at this other beautiful college, my husband and I took an evening dance class together. Yes it was peculiar. It was to try to help mend our relationship. We used to dance together a lot and thought it would be a good thing to go back to "our beginning". I think we were both so tired of the torn bond that we would try anything. Music and dance was an integral part of our relationship, we loved these things, we enjoyed doing these things together and it needed to be restored.

So there hubby and I were, dancing tango, Irish step dancing, jitterbugging, and doing some salsa. It was like Forest Gump & Jenny, we had our "peas & carrots" moment that translated to a date night once a week on Fridays. One night he even spoke with that southern drawl that all in the Gump fandom adore. He took my hand and we danced like maniacs. It was the best time in a dance class.

What made this an even stranger peculiarity is that this class was at the school "The b-fly" taught at. We never ran into her, she never saw us. I had hoped things were slowly mending between us with the passage of time. I didn't know but was curious.

One night in class, we found a flyer about the Teacher of the Year Awards coming up. My husband and I thought it would be a sweet gesture so we petitioned for "The b-fly" to win. As it turned out, she received the most votes ever. I was chosen to give her the award and so I did. However, she was very busy with her upcoming concert and couldn't receive it. I still gave a beautiful speech even though I was still petrified to speak in public. I did it and I did it afraid.

"Live". That was one of the last words my grandmother said to me before dying last year. I shared that with someone very special. Little did I know when I needed to hear it the most, that someone special would remind me what my grandmother said: "Live." That someone special remains close to my heart.

From my eyes you not only encouraged me personally, you did so with my dancing. I remember when we first met. I shared with you my past cancer battle. I thought I was just going to take a ballet class to get my body back in shape. What I was completely unprepared for was that because of you; I'd go on a journey to actually become a dancer again.

Dancing was taken from me due to a long term illness. Not many cared but you did. Whether planned or not, you'd help me fight to get back that which was stolen from me.

Sometimes you'd tell me to persevere but balance it with not being so hard on myself. You coaxed me to be more expressive when I danced and explore different movement. The day after my grandmother died I was dancing in class; you held my shoulders and looked in my eyes. I don't recall your exact words but the essence was: "Noelle, show me some expression, I know you're in there..." I heard all you said. It just took time for me to process it and not be afraid to let it out.

But what I treasure most, when there were no words...were your hugs.

You gave a key that made me realize I had to move on from the past and find my new voice as a dancer--a person. You prompted me to look inward and held me to account for my flaws. It was hard to hear, but I knew that you truly cared about me and it helped me be a better person. I in turn did the same for you to show that I too cared about you.

Because of that, I know things haven't always been perfect between us and there were times of friction. Something else my grandmother said:

That dynamic/friction she called: "iron sharpening iron." I feel that happened with us. To explain the metaphor: in its day, iron was the strongest metal used by forgers to craft swords. Once fashioned, they needed sharpening. To do that; two iron blades were rubbed together. This caused great friction to smooth out the bumps and grooves. Both blades had to be strong; both had to be iron on iron. If one was weaker metal, it'd crumble during the sharpening process.

My vision started to grow blurry, I felt as if I was going to have another one of my blind spells come on. I squinted hard to finish the speech—I was determined.

Being human, that "sharpening" can be difficult to endure, but the end result is two finely crafted blades of iron that are very strong, a great support for one another and the sharpening subsides.

You are the only one who truly understands my dancing, my choreography...me. You care on many levels that are why you're an excellent teacher, I hope you realize that. I'm very proud of you and glad that you've been my teacher, my friend. I'm honored to give this to you."

With that, I was congratulated by the speech instructor as I stepped off stage, "I've been teaching here 20 years and that was the best speech I'd ever heard." I thanked him. It felt good to receive the compliments graciously instead of compulsively brushing them aside. This had always been difficult for me to do with my abuse survivor background.

I also received a thunderous applause, and a few students gathered flowers from the bouquets on the tables and gave them to me.

A student who I didn't know but she knew me softly spoke to me, "I don't know if you saw this because you were looking at your paper reading the speech, but everyone was watching you waiting for your next word. It was beautiful." It took a moment for me to absorb it completely. *Was she really saying this because she meant it, or does she want something? Were these people truly affected by my voice, my words...could this be?* After I processed that moment and what had just happened, I looked up at all the people that wanted to meet me. I guess I did have something to say and I guess my voice did matter.

As I walked past the hallway behind the large multi-purpose room auditorium, I was asked by a reporter why the teacher wasn't present. I felt my heart crash and burn and as I took in a deep breath, I said she was probably busy with her concert preparations. I was then pressured about the details of our relationship and what the problems were.

"Didn't you hear what I said in the speech? I can give you a copy of it if you don't remember. What I said covers it all. I was very clear." This reporter apparently had some background information from somewhere, but I wasn't about to delve into it.

This was the beginning and practice for what would come not too far in the future but unbeknownst to me at that time. My dancer, Carol, was with me and knew everything I had done that day, the situation, the relationship friction between myself and "The b-fly", and how public speaking troubled me. She said I handled all of it very well and hugged me. I let her hug me and wasn't afraid. I had always been afraid of close relationships after being so dreadfully wounded.

Then knowing that sometimes your heart can be broken in just that certain way, that no one can put it back together…except maybe one special person.

It was like a baby breathing for the first time whenever I was on the other college campus, no judgment, no fear, no horrific past, just fun and dancing. The grassy hills and peaceful atmosphere was a stress-reducer even with my heavy class load. Time waited for no one and I wasn't getting younger, but I was getting better. Sadly, my stay there was soon coming to a close. My degree almost completed, and I was going to take advantage of everything I could to further my rehabilitation.

Professional Master Classes were often held at this college. One of my favorite ones was with Patrick Frantz who was Premier

Danseur with the Paris Opera Ballet at age 22, Artistic Director for his own Los Angeles area dance company: La Danserie, and has had an accomplished career as artiste and choreographer. Judy Pissaro-Grant who worked with him as Resident Choreographer for La Danserie and Administrative Director was also there and an amazing lady. I loved working with these people so much. Intense but encouraging, strong in technique and open with praises.

During tech week in which we set the lighting design and rehearsed our dances on stage, Mr. Frantz watched my dance. He told me that he enjoyed it very much and to "keep it up". I would remember these words whenever discouragement came my way. He was well pleased. I think he saw every run-through of my piece that week leading up to the performances. I had the privilege to study under Mr. Frantz and Judy upon occasion in other Master Classes, classes and workshops. I studied one-on-one with Judy for quite a time to help me perfect my ballet technique. An immense honor to receive tutelage from someone(s) with technique directly from Paris Opera Ballet. For me, this was a highpoint for me. It's important to have exquisite training and education when it comes to ballet. I currently pass this technique onto my students.

Fate is a complex thing in theory and practicality. As you know, I wanted very much to be able to present a dance at the consortium in L.A. One year later—this happened for me; I would perform at the consortium that I had been an audience member at the year prior. My mentor invited me to present "Red Ribbons" uncensored in this venue. My dancers and I said yes. I did not cajole, beg, barter, manipulate the powers that be, or plead, it was just my time/our time to dance our heavy message to that audience.

It coincidentally was the same day that we opened our show at the college's performing arts center. I was overwhelmed with joy and great fear. Joy because I got my wish. Fear because I knew "The b-fly", my former instructor from the other college, would be there. She would know that I was attending this other college and she would see my dance as intended and uncensored.

If I didn't know any better, I would have guessed that my life was a perfectly scripted story with irony, jeopardy, joy and contradiction. I looked upward and shook my head. There would be no butterfly to caress my cheek inside this auditorium, but perhaps another provision would substitute. If only I could put it in the proper perspective at that time.

We arrived and indeed, "The b-fly" was there. I was shaken and wanted to be invisible at that time. If she didn't know that I was attending this other college, she knew then. I prayed that she would be comforted. It wasn't a moment of vindication because I never saw her as my enemy. It was a moment of grief. On the outside I projected confidence and conquest.

The fact was: I was afraid. I kept trying to "Breathe"; almost hyperventilating. I wanted to bolt, she held my hand so tight—she wasn't going to let me leave and said so. The summary of it went down like this, "Cut the crap Noelle, we're doing this." I had to chuckle a bit, I loved the strength in this woman and I loved her for being real with me. If it had not come from a place of love, which it did, I don't think I would've appreciated her sentiment as much. Currently, when I feel like bolting, I replay her exact words and tone in my head and I do not bolt. I remain firmly planted and do the job that needs to be done no matter what.

We must remember: Life begins where fear ends.

My group danced brilliantly and I gave of myself generously to the audience in my performance. "The b-fly" had finally seen the dance as it was intended. Knowing that wore me down emotionally. That was all I had left in me as a human being and I left the performance area weak-kneed and somehow triumphant. She drove my SUV back to our college so we could perform our emotionally draining piece "again" that day.

She warned me not to watch the film insert, she knew how it triggered me, but despite her wisdom, I watched it, and lost it on stage. The performance was monumental, but I was an irreparable mess.

At the end of the day, she found me collapsed in the hallway. I had had it; too many raw emotions from all angles in one day. She found my husband and he drove us home. Three people in the audience walked out on us and the heartbreaking thing wasn't that they didn't want to see my dance or that it was a rejection, but that they missed on opportunity to heal or help another heal, and then possibly the most tragic of all: a teaching opportunity to help prevent further molestation incidents. I left all of that at the foot of fate. Time would dictate and be responsible for an outcome in their lives, it wasn't for me to own. Some people are not ready and I had to respect that. I did my job. I made them feel something. That was all I could do.

Subsequent performances were handled better. I met and greeted the audience after the show.

One particular exchange that I still treasure was when a mother approached me with her young daughter. She shared that she had a "talk" with her daughter about my piece and what the dance meant. I bent down to the little girl. She was sweet and meek, but there was a power in her beautiful smile and soft gaze. I saw my eyes in her eyes.

"What did you think about my dance?"

"I won't let anyone touch me like that." The little girl spoke austerely.

I put my hand to my mouth, I was taken aback and realized that I was instrumental in seeding a small change in this young life's soul. ME?! Sick, broken, hurt, confused, petite, little, me could impress upon others and move their hearts. How could this be? But it was this way. This was my truth.

My throat choked slightly with tears as I nodded my head. She embraced me and kissed my cheek. Her mother thanked me as the rest of the audience piled out and many came my way. It was followed by "Thank You", "Great work", "Do you dance anywhere else?", and a myriad of compliments.

I knew that my dancing had reached more hearts. I had

something of value to offer the public, not just entertainment, but a message of HOPE. I was astounded that I could be used for good after having so many harrowing things happen to me. I didn't think that I had any value as a human being to offer anyone anything. From that point I was COMPELLED to reach more hearts. Compelled to become a "fisher of men, women, and children" and give them tremendous HOPE of help and healing and LOVE.

The container is never the source of the water; it is the vessel in which it flowed through and carried. I wanted to be a vessel that carried nourishment to others.

There were tender people drowning in cesspools others had created for them. Their pasts haunting them much like mine had. I wanted to fish them out. I wanted to tell them with dance that they could be whole again not only survive but thrive. They may never have been told that. My calling had completely coalesced that day. Finally, I understood what I was supposed to do. The light of FAITH shone on my pathway to guide me directly to people's hearts. The next step would be made known when necessary.

By the end of that show's run, I felt I had matured spiritually in a way that is much like a treasure hunter looking for gold.

Understanding for the butterfly also became a little bit more clearer. My Red Ribbons were not only for me but for her, for those that I danced with, for countless others who lost their innocence by no fault of their own. The red ribbon would become a heralding symbol of overcoming and strength, not weakness and victimhood.

As I shared earlier, only three people ever walked out on us during this show's run, and from that point on, no one ever walked out of the performance again as it gained reputation and accolades of understanding.

CHAPTER 8

CANCER TO DANCER - LET THIS BE MY LAST BATTLEGROUND

"I'm not broken, but my heart may be frozen."

There is a beauty all around us. Some may be afraid to let it grow because of what they had to let go. Some are afraid to let it shine because of the woundings of time. Some are afraid because the world can be cruel. But I say all these things helped build a strength anew that created the deeper beauty in you. Noelle Andressen

"Awakenings & Beginnings Dance Festival" Los Angeles
ROSEWOOD Choreographed by Noelle Andressen
Photo © Brendan Bonney 2015

"Red Ribbons" would become the name of my dance company since it was the foundation in which I used to grow from. I didn't want to be common sounding by calling it Red Ribbons Dance Company (although our junior dance ensemble team is called Red Ribbons Dance Ensemble), so my husband plainly asked, how do you say red ribbons in French.

I said, "Rubans Rouges (roo – bahn – rooj)". It was perfect. I liked the catchy play-on and lend from Moulin Rouge, I was French, it sounded more artful than Red Ribbons, no one else was using it, (and why would they – it was too unique and a bit odd) it was perfect. The challenges became: marketing a French name to an American audience, not getting confused with the AIDS red ribbon, and not looking like a Christmas gift adornment. I wanted this to work and with time, patience and my strong marketing background, I'd make it work. The branding of Rubans Rouges Dance began and I still had two semesters left before I graduated with my AA degree.

With the inception of my dance company, I developed a repertoire of many dances with varying messages. There was always a fear of not being able to rise to the height I inadvertently placed this bar of achievement for myself. Still, I rose to the challenge and soared.

We created a Board with people of prestige and honor. Some were very familiar with the art world and others shrewd business men who didn't screw around. This is what I needed and loved. It was an impenetrable fortress that would not tolerate unprofessionalism, bribery, theft, blacklisting, and any of the other craziness that can occur in any industry. I knew I was protected and should one of them have failed, they would be held accountable by the law and shown no mercy. I am extremely kind, but once crossed, consider that you have just burned a bridge forever.

Another beautiful opportunity was presented to me by Tomiko Fraser Hines. She's an amazing lady, actress, and motivational speaker that I admire and had often sought counsel from. She was the first African American model/spokeswoman for Maybelline and has done many roles in TV and film. Besides being gorgeous, she had a heart that loved deeply and worked on many projects of her own.

There is so much beauty in the world, we sometimes tend to overlook it because it can be found in the subtleties of life. One of these subtleties was found in Tomiko's next project: a wonderful photo book called "UNbound". Tomiko created this collaborative work with Natiya Guin who photographed it. She had asked me and several other women to be a part of her expression.

We were all photographed solely in our raw beauty, very little makeup if any and a peach, chiffon, length of fabric was wrapped around us.

That airy, light draping was placed on our bodies in unique ways that seemed to suit each lady perfectly. Tomiko put that much care in every detail and made us all feel like goddesses. I loved how we shared the same piece of fabric. We were all woven together with the same chord and that made this project and our bond even stronger.

This is where I first was inspired with "Cancer to Dancer". I was featured as a dancer and wrote a short essay of what it meant to be UNbound and how I found beauty in myself while having had cancer. In the collage of heart touching stories and soul bearing photos by many strong and relevant women, I contributed my portion.

Both of these ladies, Tomiko and Natiya, were incredible artists to collaborate with and aimed at bringing out the inner beauty in others. Tomiko specifically showed all of us how to shine and truly helped me find my UNbound beauty. That was and still is her goal. She's a very important role model in my life. If you don't have her book, I highly recommend getting a copy or several. It's bound to touch another women's heart.

After the book's release, my dance company and I had dozens more to follow that summer. Women's healing and wellness groups contacted me to perform our quartet, we performed at Universities and on TV shows. The reaction trend was always similar: dead silence during the performance, a pause after the dance was performed, subtle applause that would build to a roaring climax. This four minute dance: RED RIBBONS, had a magic of its own and created a movement and thus my dance company: Rubans Rouges Dance was birthed. My love gift for "The b-fly" became a love gift for many and I had more to say.

One particular performance at California State University Northridge in California, surprised me. It was a charming theatre and nice sized stage being hosted by One Circle. This group was about preventing child abuse and harnessing the talents and experiences of others to further spread the word and raise awareness in hopes to stop abuse of children.

My company's mission fit in well with this group. I expanded the "Red Ribbons" vocabulary and added a second dance piece called "NUMB". It was an expression of getting to the point in your psyche where you cannot take one more breath of pain so you anesthetize yourself into numbness. It was darker in tone than "Red Ribbons", but I took the chance in presenting this to an audience. It too was well received.

After this performance many approached me and my dancers. There were mostly accolades and some tears. This piece is always accompanied with tears of relief, sorrow, grief, confusion and a release for many. One woman said that I had a huge stage presence and in chatting with me she said that it was genuine and could tell I was also genuine in person. It wasn't an act and she felt my authenticity was what amplified my natural aura. I thanked her although it's hard for me to take compliments after having been through what I had experienced.

Not being one for public speaking, I found myself jostled in front of several news reporters and video cameras. I stammered and searched for words. I didn't like talking about myself for fear of my words sounding like bragging. I also didn't want to hurt anyone, and my tongue had a history of being a double edged sword with the ability to build up and inadvertently hurt. My desire to be direct and honest can be soothing but also if timed incorrectly, an unintentional dagger. I stumbled through most of the interviews when I focused on the fear. When I concentrated on reaching people's hearts, looked into their eyes and connected, the fear dissipated and I did well.

Without placing any over significance or leaning to influence any specific spiritual direction, my massage therapist told me when lining up my chakras that my heart and voice were the two strengths in my body. I don't understand all of the new age philosophy and its meaning but I believed what he said and appreciated it. It was confirmation of what I had been told in the past by others, my fear was walking in these gifts.

Public speaking was a flaw for me and yet it was meant for me to harness and use to exhort. I hired a speaking coach and began the grueling process of overcoming and refining my raw talent to bond with people.

Getting the heart and voice to work harmoniously and flawlessly together was daunting and I teetered with giving up many times. I was a dancer. I chose that first so I wouldn't have to use words to speak. I was afraid of speaking in large groups. One on one was fine. My coach taught me proper sitting alignment, how to face the camera, when to address it directly or have my eye line meet the interviewer.

The cancer treatment destroyed my memory. Recalling words and events clearly was like cutting pieces from a fog, capturing it, and sorting through the density. The moment I gained some clarity, it would dissolve into obscurity. To help resolve this, he gave me memory games and homework to improve and reconnect the wiring in my brain.

This with an enhanced diet improved things greatly. I also enrolled in intensive and advanced professional dance classes and workshops to help my short term memorization of choreography. One of these classes was taught by Jamie Nichols who was and still is an amazing dancer and master teacher. She became one of my mentors and now colleague outside of the school setting. She guided me in so many aspects of producing as well since she had been producing Celebrate Dance for over 10 years. It was a beautiful evening of dance that brought the dance community together. My company and I attended every year except when we had performances. I also returned to my acting career and acting classes. I was now forced to memorize lines, speak in front of more than one person, and I learned to harness my "presence" or "it" factor.

Another coach of mine and friend, Duane Whitaker, who played Maynard in Pulp Fiction, worked with me to further my skills. Carolyne Barry trained me too. You would know her face as she's been in many TV shows and commercials like Start Trek The Next Generation, The Man From U.N.C.L.E., Dynasty and few other Aaron Spelling Productions. She loved dance and dancing and thought it was great that I was successful in this career although she was a bit biased and thought I should continue acting more. She forced me out of my comfort zone and into her protégé's acting improv class. She was tough, but loved each of her students and wanted them to succeed. (Sadly, Carolyne died in 2015. She struggled with breast cancer like me. She never got to see one of my concerts. Hearing of her death sent me downwards. She was and will always be a great woman who will be missed. This fueled the fire inside of me that grew to hate this disease as it consumed so many that I loved.)

While going through my Pygmalion transformation, I had a vocal coach who taught me how to graciously accept compliments and criticism. He slowed down my speech to make it more eloquent and told me to breathe.

"What did you say?" I asked him with wonder.

"Noelle, you just need to breathe." He laughed slightly.

Any time someone spoke that word (breathe) to me, it got my attention and drew me inward to reflect upon each time it was spoken to me. Time would then seemingly stop and move forward surrealistically.

That word: breathe, resurfaced at interesting times in my life and said by vastly different people. The meaning from when my husband said it to me as I was dying from cancer, was carried to the present and its meaning enlarged. It constantly saved me.

Many people went into the making and re-making of me. I was slowly being put back together and refined. However, as I said before, sometimes your heart can be broken in just that certain way that no one can put it back together except maybe one special person.

As I was thinking about this and walking to my SUV, I thought about the "The b-fly" who started with me along in my journey. Then at that moment, a yellow swallow tail flew over my head. I looked upward and smiled. I wondered how she was doing. Then it dawned on me that any time I thought of her, I would see a butterfly. I then started referring to her as just that: a butterfly whose wings were ready but she had not come out of her chrysalis.

My eyes watered and I shunned from my thoughts. Was I missing her? The place in which the thorn of love was burrowed began to ache. Yes, I think I did miss her. With that, I was inspired to create another beautiful piece for the following summer: "The Silent Rose". The inspiration: that beautiful piece of fabric from "The b-fly's" photo.

Many holidays passed without Nana while I was working on my dance career and company. One afternoon I pined to hear her voice. I wrote a journal entry on social media:

December 3, 2011
if I close my eyes really tight...
If I close my eyes really tight I can still see her face...it was the last time I'd see her...she knew and I knew it'd be the last time I'd see her...on this earth... Her heart belonged to god--I will see her again. I just miss her dreadfully so. Missing her more this time of year...

I remember where I was when my cell alerted me. I knew it was my brother calling me to tell me of her passing....I couldn't answer it--avoiding the truth--I kept speaking to the person I was with. When I got home I listened to the voice mail that confirmed my fears

If I cover my ears with my hands really close I can still hear her voice calling me angel...

I loved spending Christmas with her and celebrating the birth of our lord. I will use this time to celebrate all that was good...

The mourning process was taking longer than I desired. It hurt to breathe, it hurt to stand still, it hurt to think about her and it hurt not to think about her. I couldn't win. I had no peace.

It was with the furtherance of my dance company that I completely realized all the horror I had suffered through in my short life could be redeemed by helping others. Some people work as counselors, some are doctors, some are authors, and then there was me, a dancer. I used dancing to help people. I tackled heady subjects such as death, miscarriage, abortion, cancer, and many other social issues. Our following of fans grew and I found myself leading a small group of dancers to venues and places I didn't think I'd ever see. "Red Ribbons-Shattered Innocence" remained the top requested repertoire piece.

Rubans Rouges Dance continued to grow in its members and reputation. We performed in St. Barbara, Mexico, San Diego, Monterey, New York City, Brooklyn, Las Vegas, Temecula, San Marcos, all over Los Angeles and Hollywood. I was nominated for Performance Artist of the Year in 2012 and made it to the finalists with my dance partner.

Financially speaking, we were still recovering from the negative effects treating cancer can have on a family. The emotional wound healing was in progress, but monetarily, things were not easily remedied. Imagine being lost in a dark labyrinth with no light, no clues, no map, and having to solve the riddle while physically stunted. It seemed impossible. At times it was. Each new venue we performed at presented more hurdles than normal. If we traveled out of town, we had to find where we could stay that was affordable and didn't have toxins; that was a problem.

Fundraising took on more creative elements than our dance pieces at times. I taught hundreds of dance classes to fund the company. When we had successful shows the funds went to paying people and into the company at the end of each show. We found ways to barter, borrow, and in the very early days baby sit; but you do what you have to do to make things happen. As time progressed we had charity fundraising galas, special showcase performances, donors and grants.

We had amazing opportunities and saw some of the greatest sights. There's a beautiful country out there, if only we took the time to view it.

As my company started to tour, we were all getting very fatigued. It had taken its toll on all of us and a few of my dancers had to resign because of other life commitments. Losing anyone saddens me greatly, I get attached, I fall in love with all people, especially my dancers. At this point my board and I decided that I should perform alone or do trios or duets. It would be more economical and lessen my responsibilities.

During the submission process to venues and festivals, 70 percent of the acceptances were for my solo pieces. They liked my dancers and my ensemble pieces, but they wanted me, no matter how hard I tried to persuade them otherwise. My mentors encouraged me to do large cast pieces, this was confusing since as a mentee you trust your mentors' judgments. However, my board wanted me to grow and couldn't grasp why some of my mentors didn't understand that people wanted to see me. Nana often said to give of myself and don't hold back selfishly. "Noelle, they came to see you and want to feel your presence. They want to feel your experience."

The board laid out the pros and cons for me going solo, at least for a time. There was nothing negative about my performing solo except one thing: this petrified me. I was fine in a group, and since that 2007 ballet performance at that college, I never got nervous as long as I wasn't alone on stage. Performing solo was a skill I needed to develop. My board knew that. They also knew that when I was on stage, eyes went to me.

My board somehow convinced me to try doing a solo. I had already performed one in a "test-run" at a college, and it went well save for my anxiety attacks. The instructors were extremely supportive of me and wanted to see me do well.

During our board meeting, I let out a sigh and nodded my head reluctantly. Okay, I would try taking the solo "Gethsemane" on the road. I had laughed at the irony of it all. The word Gethsemane has a few meanings: it comes from a Hebrew/Aramaic word Gat Shemanim. It means a pressing of oils or oil press. In ancient days, olives were pressed between two large stones until it was refined into oil. It was a threshing floor in many ways. The title is used metaphorically as an abstracted connection how a human soul can be pressed and pressed until it finally has no other choice but to make a decision to succumb or over-come. In order to survive, one must over-come.

The symbolism in the title of my piece, the meaning of the word and what I personally was experiencing was similar. I very much felt like my heart was being squeezed and pressed. This would also become more significant in a few months later that year, perhaps a foreshadowing of my life events that would cruelly unfold.

The first professional venue I presented this piece was in Santa Barbara at Center Stage Theatre. Intimate, but not too small. It was big enough to scare the hell out of me. One of my sweetest and spunkiest mentors encouraged me deeply. I then performed it at one of my dear friend's festivals in St. Monica at The Miles Playhouse.

As I traveled along my creative road, I developed and added to this piece in length and thought. I changed the name to "Decision". I felt that depicted the piece more and conveyed my deepest heart about it all. There always comes a time in life when we must make a "decision". I also didn't want it to sound overly religious, although a viewer could extract that valid meaning from it as well.

Another mini-festival in a black box theatre in Pasadena produced by my mentor, provided an opportunity to dance this solo again. I had dozens of comforting arms around me to hold me from exploding or imploding; as it often felt like my insides were quaking with nausea and fear.

The lights went out, the theatre was dark and the magic began. My solo would be up soon and my Nana's soothing voice came to me in my need like a sweet vision, "Angel, are you afraid?" I found myself biting my bottom lip and nodding my head. "Then do it afraid. You will not break. You will become stronger." Reminiscing about my Nana brought a calming salve to my anxiety. A mentor of mine also had this effect on me and said something similar.

It is always important to remember that your feet know the way and will guide you in the midst of a storm. Even though the storms that came my way would throw me off balance, my feet knew the way and would meet the floor and guide me. I ferociously performed my solo. At first, I never see the audience but they see me. I feel them and I make them feel me and what I'm expressing on stage in the moment of passion. After my bow, I ran off stage and vomited in the bathroom sink backstage. Tears often followed. I was done. It was done. It was done well. Vomit prevention would become a continual growth process. I could only think of one person that may be able to cure me of this; the butterfly, but she was not there.

One of my colleagues tapped their knuckles on the door and asked if I was okay. I didn't know how to answer that, yes I was okay but I needed to get a hold of this problem. I was a professional dancer beleaguered by what amounted to as butterflies in my stomach. I felt childish.

She came in and stroked my back.

"What happened?" She asked.

"It's really stupid, but I get nervous when I'm by myself because when I was around 14 I had a guy stalking me. He was a voyeur creeper kinda guy. Long story but I have a bad reaction when this type of thing happens. I'm fine though."

I wiped my brow and fixed my face and we greeted the audience in the foyer.

A gentleman approached me and introduced himself as a director-producer. I hadn't heard of him before, I came from a strong film background and knew a lot of the names in the business and worked with some. He wanted to use me in his next dance film.

He said he hoped I'd come out, he wanted to meet me. He had asked several people who the redhead was. Everyone he asked presented another redheaded dancer to him. She had the prettiest strawberry-blonde hair (my natural color), she was a good, technical, dancer. No one thought to share my name; not even my mentors. This was odd. He said, "No not that redhead, the "Red Head"! He told me that the other one was good but that I was great.

I was intrigued but also told him that I don't do film any more but would consider his offer. It was a paid production and I wanted to find out more. We had many meetings and he eventually won me over. I loved his concept. He hired me to do the choreography and dance. Contracts and all things were put in place and a film was about to be made.

With each performance I did either solo or with my dancers, our reputation continuously grew, especially in Los Angeles. I had people who I didn't know come up to me on the street and say that they saw me dance and would ask for a selfie two-shot or an autograph. It was strange at first because I'm just a small town girl that lives in the big city who has a country girl heart. I tended to shy away from this type of thing. I did my best to be gracious and friendly. I often turned the attention on them and wanted to earnestly get to know them as human beings. I'm much better one-on-one as I said, I liked to find out what I could do to help others.

As long as there weren't any voyeurs around I was all right, but then how would I really know if one was around. I had experienced a taste of fame throughout my life. Each time I pushed it away. Notoriety caused me to feel as if others owned me and left little time for myself. I was always being scheduled to go, to do, to be something or somewhere. Often, I would step outside and seek solitude from the "noise".

When this happened, I would think: "This is a moment in my day when I own myself I don't answer to anyone at that time and I can still hear my heart beating…it's still there…I'm still breathing…I'm not broken, but my heart may be frozen." I was undoing the damage within.

One of our company's favorite commissioned works was for a Passion Play at an enormous church. The auditorium seated over 1,500 and we performed at least 10 times. This was our biggest audience for our company yet. By the end of the show's run, we had performed our gift of love for over 10,000 people. We portrayed angels and danced in two sections of this theatrical, multi-media, play depicting the passion week in the Bible. I was asked to do a solo for a flashback sequence depicting the birth of a- baby in a manger. I agreed and was terrified. Again, stating simply: I didn't like doing solos. They assured me that there would be two other people on stage portraying Joseph and Mary. They wouldn't be dancing, but acting. It gave little comfort. I did it. I did it afraid. My performance was en pointe and I busted out consecutive turns from fifth flawlessly. I just didn't like the feelings of all eyes on me and the butterflies in my stomach.

One of the nights I looked out into the audience to try to see them. I was curious who was out there. On my way over towards center stage in the middle of a jeté, I was able to stop and take a dramatic pause. It was too dark to see most of them but I did see a beautiful young girl in the front row which was extremely close to the stage. Even with my poor eyesight I saw her big eyes staring at me. I wondered if I was inspiring her to become a dancer, or was she already dreaming of doing it. I remembered the first time I saw a ballerina on stage, I was in awe. These were the eyes that were now looking up at me. Quickly, I got over myself and my fears for that moment and I finished my dance just for her. We never know whose hearts we may touch with our deeds and words. It was the best I performed that section.

During the blackout I walked to my spot and held it for five seconds until I knew the stage was clear for me to exit. I had been so deep in the moment that I didn't quite make it to my mark in holding my position and when I swung around, I found my right hand that was along my side suddenly immersed in water. I took one more step and had my "I Love Lucy" moment as I half way fell into the baptismal tub. They didn't drain it. The set was built around it since it sat off to the side of the stage where I exited.

One other funny not-so-funny moment happened on the night the fog machine was working overtime and we danced down the flight of stairs onto the stage we couldn't see very well. One of my dancers said, "Noelle what do we do?" I knew she was referring to having to do our turns and the spotting issue. I spoke loud enough for her to hear me, "the light!" We had to spot a light from off stage to keep our bearings. The fog kept building to the point that the audience couldn't even see us or anything occurring on stage. We cut our performance short for the sake of safety and fumbled in the fog to grab each other's hands. We had to do two chassé steps to where we believed the Christ was. You could hear a voice say "over here." It was great live theater.

When all went well, this was the most enrapturing moment for me. Not many get to dance through a fog as the Christ was about to roll away the stone to show His resurrection. The music, the audience, the scenery, the costumes and textures, it was magical and felt like being in the garden of Gethsemane. I don't consider myself a "religious" person and don't have prejudices against any religion or faiths, but I have to admit that this final scene of the resurrection was very powerful. To see someone who was dead rise again is breath taking. The voices of over one hundred cast members singing were ominous and victorious. That was an amazing crescendo and we ended our victory dance posing around Jesus. Interesting fact, I knew this young gentleman portraying

Jesus would go on to pastor a church someday in the future; and he did several years later along with his beautiful wife.

This was an incredible honor to partake in and everyone so pleased with our performance, well most everyone.

Some people had a difficult time accepting dance performance. Keep in mind this wasn't for a church service, a baptism, or "entertainment". This was 6 beautiful women, all with a faith based backgrounds doing ballet in very modest white flowing dance gowns, white leotards and tights underneath; there was nothing scant or sexual about this piece. This was not an exhibition of the body, or pelvic gyration. This was beautifully executed classical ballet technique. Rumor had it that it was some of the elders who had a conniption about it all. The audience loved it and became dedicated friends of our company and completely supported us. I close this paragraph with a scripture reference for those who are too rigid to see the beauty: "They leapt and danced before The Lord." Most likely it was Davidic dancing, but I'm fairly certain that The Lord, if He even cared, was well pleased with our ballet performance.

In the midst of the successful Southern California tours and performances, my mom called and told me she was selling her boat and moving back to Vegas. I was ecstatic and curious as to why the big rush to get back home. I hadn't seen her since Nana passed on. She would be near and we could finally do many things together. We began to make plans for our upcoming dance festival that

January and she wanted to help sew costumes for my company. We would have quality bonding time that we both longed for. This was too many years overdue, that in the past she would evade and caused me to become fatigued with chasing her.

Mom habitually ran away from situations and people, she never stopped running. Any time I mentioned it she'd switch the subject, "Mom, what are you running from--"

"Are you still teaching dance classes?" She just wouldn't address it.

I wanted to tell her to: Be free but don't run. One heals the past, the other relives the past.

There was a deep desire to be closely connected to her again. I loved her smile, her voice, her hugs. Everything!

It is somewhat of an analogy: The rose still loves the butterfly, even though it leaves to migrate for the eventual winter. The love is there somewhere buried beneath the decay of the autumn leaves. Woundings and past hurts can be like autumn leaves—they're signs of death. It was a withering on the vine-branches. Something has changed and broken off but this isn't always a bad or negative thing. It's a sign of life yet to come. Seeing a butterfly with the wispy wintery winds subtly appearing, is a sign of winter on the way and it's a reminder of what will come next: a rebirth in spring. The rose blooms, the butterflies get their wings, and life grows again. So even though it may seem like a dark and cold winter on the way, the rose will always remember the love of spring and the joys of the butterfly.

Something had changed this time between mom and I and she was coming home. Maybe she finally stopped running. You never win by running. You win by fighting and being a warrior. She truly was a warrior, I think she just needed to be reminded of that.

My son and I took a walk that afternoon and he asked me when the last time was I prayed for my mom; he knew I prayed for the butterfly more. I said that I stopped praying for her years ago. I gave up. I became weary. He said that I should start praying for her again. It wasn't too late for us to have a good relationship. I took our son's advice and asked God to soften her heart.

My son saw a butterfly pass overhead. "Mom, look, a butterfly."

It was a Monarch spreading its vibrant orange wings. I thought of another woman's heart along with my mother's that day.

It was still hot as the Fall of 2012 approached. I was training with two very intense choreographer-dancers during this time to get me physically ready for the independent dance film. We were scheduled to shoot in November with the gentleman and his wife that had seen me perform in the Pasadena show. He had a very professional crew, lovely assistants, and his costumer extremely talented. We had several rehearsals, fittings, photo shoots, and meetings about the details. Every day I stayed disciplined, watched my health, diet and weight. I built up my stamina and strength and did the best I could to overcome the insomnia that started to plague me. I carried on with my routine.

September 18, 2012, I had purchased Painted Lady caterpillars. I wanted to witness the lifecycle of a butterfly with my own eyes and be a part of the mystery of transformation. I questioned mortality, life, and how beings can change whether it was from creation being birthed or the life essence being taken away.

The fascinating aspect of evolution piqued my curiosity and I wanted to harness more understanding for these almost mythical creatures that haunted and taunted me at times with their presence. Their transcendent like qualities gave insight into the divine.

What was life and did we choose to start or stop breathing or was it chosen for us? How did people change and what elements would catapult them to change? I felt as if the butterfly could show me an answer. I was a visual person, maybe if I could see the answer, it would help me. I had already choreographed a piece called "The Silent Rose" which was about a rosebud afraid to bloom and a butterfly learning how to use its wings. The metamorphosis and life-cycle fascinated me as an artist.

September 19, my brother called me. He asked briefly how I was doing and got to the point of his phone call rather urgently. Our mom was in the hospital. Mom wasn't one to go to the doctor for anything. She would never do it or go to the hospital unless it was dire. I nervously fidgeted with the drawstring on my sweats. I frantically asked my brother if mom was alive and what happened. He said she was alive and he didn't know a lot; he didn't want to worry me as he knew how I was. I could tell he was more concerned about me and how I was taking the news so he worked on redirecting me to the positive.

"Let's wait for the test results. Noelle, you ok?" I was quiet while my brother waited on the phone for my reaction.

"Yeah…" I barely whispered. "Yeah, I'm ok. I got this. Call me when you hear more. Can I call mom? I can call her. Yeah, I'll call mom, what hospital—what room is she in?"

He told me she's in the E.R. but I could try calling in a couple days. He said he'd let me know what was going on. I felt that he wasn't fessing up everything but I didn't want to press him. We hung up and I was a wreck. I had just talked to her, she was just in San Diego for my niece's birthday. She was fine and she was going to be fine as I had convinced myself. I told my son and husband what had happened. We did the only thing we felt we could do: PRAY. What else do you do when things are out of your control? I also grabbed my favorite wine and had a quick glass.

I posted on my Facebook wall that my mom needed prayers. I wasn't ready to let her go and hoped that it wasn't a major health problem.

Nana (left) could easily have been a screen goddess. She was gorgeous. Mom (right) stunning child. We referred to this as the Gerber Baby photo. Both beauties. Nana (below) a dancing majorette. Very flexible. I have a photo of me like this on line. Facebook.com/RubansRougesDance

Nana's Mom, Anna, is the bride (Top). Quite the scandal then. Italians & Sicilians marrying was a faux pas. Her brothers and sisters (23 total not all pictured): Joselina, Josemina, Josefina, you get the idea The gentleman bottom row furthest right is part Egyptian and Sicilian. I have African blood in my heritage. Cool beans!

(Middle) one of the homes I lived in on Union Street. Back right window was my room. The garage was where Nana & I made our stage. (Bottom) Lindberg Grade School. Looks nothing like this now.

It must be love. This was at Carluccio's Italian Restaurant in Las Vegas. My aunt Diane and Uncle Paul took us out for our 5th wedding anniversary. We love Disney films. Can you guess which one we're emulating?

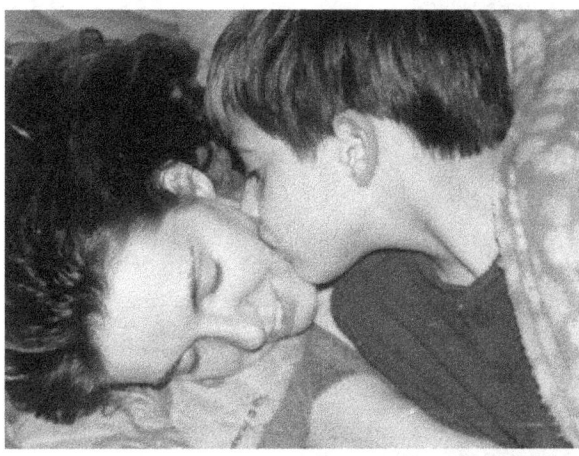

This is our son taking care of me when I was very sick. He always snuggled up with me and got whatever I needed. Sometimes he would dance and jump around to make me smile.

My husband and our son. There was always music of some kind in our home. My husband was working on a music score that earned him an Emmy nomination in 2004. Our wee one decided to crawl underneath and join in.

Mom was a bit of a daredevil at times. This is her sky-diving. I'm pretty adventurous but this wouldn't be something I'd try. Kudos to you mom! I'm still working on the Ferris Wheel/heights issues.

Mom was such a beauty in her high school grad photo. I'm in both shots. "Baby me" (left). You can see my strawberry blonde hair in the original shot. "Embryo me" (right). Mom was a couple months pregnant with me. Apparently that Easter was very fertile ;)

Mom & I at Dee & Gandalf's (yes it's his real name! Awesome!) wedding. They were friends of our family and still are. Mom's cute little bobbed hairstyle which she wore most of her life. She would change it up to suit the decade. She only had it super long during the late 70s and looked just like Arwen in TLOTR. She also reminded a lot of people of Princess Leia.

Rubans Rouges Dance's first company photo-shoot. It took two hours. We did a lot of acro-yoga at the time. (top left: me, Kim, Nick, Milton). (bottom) Jamie Nichols choreographed a very expressive dance for a summer workshop. It was an honor for me to dance for her since she seldom choreographed for performances. One of the best contemporary artists I've worked with who mentored me.

(top) One of my favorite photos and moments from "Red Ribbons" with Kristine Purcell at the Moorpark Performing Arts Center. This 50 minute dance piece was the epic flagship that started my dance company. (below) We were angels in The Passion Play. This was moment before the fog kicked in. It was a gorgeous set designed and over 100 cast members. Privilege to be a part of a moving production.

(top) This was a site specific piece Nick and I did. It was fun to explore the terrain and each other's movements. (below) Nick, Orlando, me. This became one of our most well-known photos when we were first starting out touring. We had quite an ensemble of 7 truly diverse movers, dancers, and actors. We always had a great time.

(top) Orlando and I. Dancing outdoors has been a staple for the company. We all love nature and tend to be mindful of the environment. You can see "Natural Beauty" on our youtube channel. https://www.youtube.com/user/RedRibbonsDance

(below) Carol & I. She adopted me when my mom died. We've been dancing together for 9 years. I love her deeply.

I'm just a small town girl that lives in the big city who has a country girl heart. (top) me

All these photos were taken by Jared Kale. Rubans Rouges Dancers work hard and play hard.

We also love each other's company. Just hanging around before a performance. (left) Nick & me.

Ornlando & Nick on the beach before a show. Nick is one of our flyers. Orlando is always a strong supportive base.

Showing off the gams. In between our matinee and evening repertoire shows, we like to lay around and take in the theater atmosphere. Feels good to accomplish some good.

Rehearsals are arduous tasks but my dancers are delights and make it smooth going. We enjoy each other's company during work and play.

(top) me, (middle) Orlando & Carol work on their duet from "Red Ribbons". The two of them together have immense chemistry. Both great emote-ers.

(below) Me signing checks for stipends. We had to work hard to get to the point where we could pay stipends and our crew. It seems that is the most challenging item for art based companies to manage. We're glad that we arrived at this point. We love all dancers, our dance community, the stage and crew workers, all of them dearly. The least we can do is offer an honorarium or stipend.

Some shots our son took of me. He seems to get the intricacies of my choleric-melancholy personality and captures interesting nuances.

The middle one I love deeply because it was shot in the rain in the freezing cold February air. I jumped outside and got soaked. I often rain-dance because it feels so freeing to have the water cascade down your body. I AM a mermaid.

(bottom) Often, I step outside and seek solitude from the "noise". When this happened, I would think: "This is a moment in my day when I own myself I don't answer to anyone at that time and I can still hear my heart beating…it is still there…I am still breathing…I am not broken, but my heart may be frozen." I was undoing the damage within. As I travel further along my career, it's a challenge to be able to hear my own voice distinguished from others in the midst of all that I have to do.

(top) Photo © Brendan Bonney for our 5 year company anniversary showcase at Live Arts LA. It was a mini-milestone and I wanted to honor my long standing dancers & my mentors. I make most of the costumes and the pink one is a fav!

(middle) ADaPT Festival 2011 dress rehearsal © Jared Kale. Our ensemble doing COMMUNION. A piece about acceptance no matter what you do, think, practice. Not in a religious sense but a community sense.

(below) Begotten. © Jared Kale. A site specific duet that we re-set on stage. We loved working with fabric. It was fun to explore the terrain underneath fabric.

Photos Jared Kale (top) ARC. (middle) Lula Washington's Dance Day Festival. (below) One of my mentor's athletic moves. I was so thrilled when I was finally able to do this. Practice makes better and stronger.

Both of these shots are behind the scenes from ENTROPY. My mom had just died and I was a wreck. The exhaustion from the emotional state of being wore me out. I was on time, professional, knew my choreography, all of it went smoothly and was a delight to be a part of. A very Bowie-esque pose as a tribute to him. His artistry has influenced a lot of mine. There's a little: "Hunky Dory" & "Heroes" album cover flavor.

(top)This was makeup design I did for a piece about the seasons of a relationship. I portrayed winter. This was done in 2009, long before the Disney film FROZEN came out. You can see some snowflake designs on my cheek that look just like when Anna, another red-head like me, was turning to ice at the end of the film. Interesting, yes.

Denise Gibson nudged me to give this makeup design a shot for my solo STORM. It was amazing and she was amazing in guiding me to create this makeup. I love David Bowie and am highly influenced by his artistry in costume & makeup.

These are random heart-felt moments that evoke a certain emotion. Another lighting technique we use are Silhouettes. It's a very dramatic statement. This is my firebird. I have a psoas injury which prevents more flexibility but it's greatly improved. Still working it.

Taken in the wings during "Red Ribbons". In this scene, the father plagues the daughter's memory when he sexually abused her. Its harsh reality never erased. The daughter has difficulty reaching out to others but her lover keeps trying. It's the memory of her father raping her that keeps a wedge between her and her lover.

It's the small things that amount to universal changes & puts forth a remedy to sway things old & new. Without these elements that compound & accumulate, our truths may never be found & yet somehow they find us if we falter on our quest. The universe beckons us to delve into the vastness of the universal truths & explore.

People who mean a lot to me…

My current partner Albertossy & I dancing "Coeur de Verre". 2015 © Brendan Bonney. My partial loss of eyesight has made this piece more challenging to do.

Anna Djanbazian, whom I adore is a Master Teacher, choreographer, and incredible lady. She's very strong and loving. She keeps me focused and keeps me tough. She sets my heart straight if I get worried. Love you Anna!

Carol, my dancer, my friend, my "mom". She takes care of me and I take care of her. We worked on this dance piece right after my mom passed. It's titled "Beloved" and is a section in the "Red Ribbons" saga.

Photos © Brendan Bonney We love to play with shapes and design. The two shots above was from UNITY during our performance. The top shot looks like a crown which was intentional. (below) an in studio photo-shoot with Brendan Bonney. I was put to the challenge to do something en pointe without pointe shoes. Voila! At least I know my toes are working properly. Bad A$$ Ballerina!

These are various shots of my other half, my husband & I. (top) doing tech work for the show. It seems glamorous to people when they think all I do is dance on stage & greet people afterwards. That's a small fraction of it. I work very hard, manually lifting things, running chords, assembling the lights, I don't go home until the floors are swept, the bathrooms are cleaned, and the equipment loaded out. I wear all hats, whatever it takes to get the job done. We have a great team & crew on board along with our tough board members.

My husband & I met on the Bob Hope McCallum Stage in Palm Desert. We used to dance together and as you can see in these fun shots, we still have the moves. Although he doesn't dance much any longer, he scores the emotional rich tapestry of music in which we dance to. Music + Dance = Harmonious Marriage.

Dress provided by Terani Couture © 2016

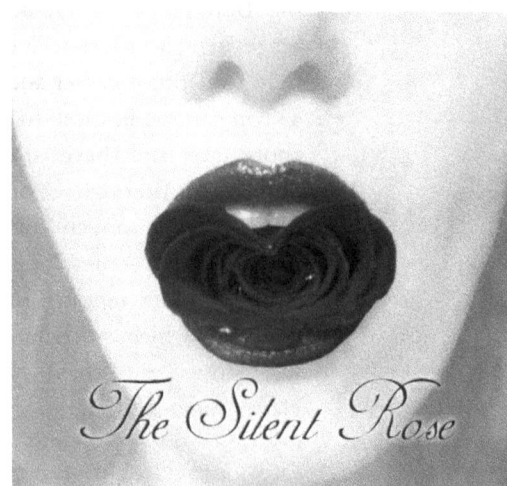

(top) from Fight for Love. I had been labeled these names. Labels are for clothes not people. I danced my scars in front of the people who hurt me. It was a powerful statement. They needed to "SEE" their words on me. This is exactly what it felt like to bare their words. I was triumphant and overcame. (left) The Silent Rose is about finding your voice - no longer silent.

My partner Albertossy & I danced at Lula Washington's Dance Theater to honor Jeremiah Tatum when he passed away in 2015. We both knew him. He was a delightful soul that we loved. Rubans Rouges did a sweet memorial for him during our repertoire show. So many in the community loved him & miss him. "Be encouraged and know the fruit of your labor will grow." Noelle Rose Andressen. Both photos © Jared Kale

(top) The "Y-Split". We named this move from our duet "Coeur de Verre". It's tricky & intense core strength needed. We've let go a couple of times when our grip slipped. It's a beautiful move that we love to do. This piece was first performed in 2010 and choreographed in 2009. Over 18 photographers to date have photographed it. (below) photo Jared Kale, another one of our performances with Kristine, Tiffany, Carol & I.

SNOW. This isn't a small section from Nutcracker, it is a small section from "Fight for Love" in which a remnant group fights a dystopian society for the freedom to love whom they choose. It's tone and themes stem from the Third Reich and the snow can be seen as ashes from burning bodies. My husband scored the Celtic flavored soundscape for this piece.

Danced by Tiffany & I. Choreographed by Noelle Andressen Photos © Brendan Bonney 2016

Terani Couture has been a great sponsor of ours. We love wearing their designs and profusely thank them for their help and support.

This was our VIP Red Carpet Gala for the opening night of "Awakenings & Beginnings Dance Festival" 2016.

When working with the designers and my board to figure out which dress would be appropriate, this was the one they decided on. I'm not going to lie—this is an amazing experience and it does feel good to wear something this fabulous. You can see all the wonderful companies, photos, and behind the scenes candid shots at facebook.com/RubansRougesDance

(left) is a lovely gown also by Terani Couture that I tried on for the infamous photo-shoot with Lois Greenfield. Again, a poor suburban girl like me never dreamed of being donned in something this exquisite. Please don't give up on your dreams.

After the Lois Greenfield shoot, Jay and I decided to take a victorious horse drawn carriage ride around Central Park in NYC. That was fun beyond fun. We both couldn't believe what had just happened. Hard & ethical work does pay off.

I just wanted to be able to say that I danced on top of the Empire State Building. So I did it. (left)

Albertossy & I during a prep for a photo-shoot for "Fight for Love". One of the most creative expressions from the entire production staff, crew, and artists. We loved every minute. Photo © Jared Kale 2015 (below).

My son, my Samwise, who carried me every step of the way through my fight for my life through the battle for my dreams coming true.

His hands are so strong and so is his heart. He has never disappointed me. He dances with me only occasionally in my company. This was a precious duet he and I did titled: "I'm Still With You". It delves deeply into how he almost lost me, his mother, to cancer. This is the nightmare he would have about losing me. (top)

I want you to "Feel the Experience". If you feel nothing, you didn't fail or get it wrong--I have failed at my job as a dancer, choreographer, a dreamer, communicator. It's not that I want you to feel any specific way. Any way you feel is good and valid. I just don't want to leave you empty handed after you've been on a dance drama journey with me and not have been moved at all. Some have misunderstood what I meant by this—clarifying it. Our facebook page & website has many videos with us discussing this fascinating concept. We LOVE our audiences! "Be free to breathe so that you believe anything is possible.

"Be free to breathe so that you believe anything is possible." (C) 2015 "Dance Warrior" excerpt Noelle Andressen

CHAPTER 9
SIX WEEKS
··•♥ ♂|♀ ♥•··

"You cannot catch the wind my friends. You can only hope to have it touch you and move you to feel something."

The very thing that caused the caterpillar to die is the very thing that caused the butterfly to fly. Noelle Andressen

"In loving memory. Mommy, I'll never let you go.
© Noelle Andressen 2012

The caterpillars arrived at a peculiar time in my life on September 21. It was a remarkable sight to see and would act as a welcomed diversion. Not only were they a spectacle, but they ate like horses. Their food granules were devoured, which made sense because they had a lot of growing and changing to do. I wondered if the caterpillar knew that it would become a beautiful butterfly. They were specially placed on a mantle in our hallway. It would become their new home. It was fun to watch them wiggle around as they burrowed into their food. They were incredibly hungry little guys.

My mom's condition loomed over my head. I worked on choreography with my beautiful dance partner Heather to get my mind off of things. We had a performance in a few weeks.

September 23, Aaron called me. The tests came back. Mom had congenital heart failure. She had an effusion around her heart, too much fluid was drowning her organ. That was fairly hard news to absorb. He also said that she had surgery. They had to cut open her chest. I sunk to the floor stunned. I knew he wasn't telling me everything the other day.

All I could picture was my mom's precious, little heart being cut open. It upset me that was done to her but understood that sometimes these things have to occur to save someone. Still I believed everyone is worth saving until their final breath. Again, not everything was told to me, I knew that, everyone was trying to spare me the details but I wanted to know more than broad strokes. That was my mom.

The problem solver in me engaged, "Okay, we need to take care of her when she gets home. I'll come out and help. Vegas is four hours away and I know about a heart diet that may help. Whatever it takes, we can do this."

While we were talking, I posted on his Facebook wall Dr. Ornish's "Reversing Heart Disease" book and the link. *"This is the book I was talking about…maybe it can help mom if it's not too late? She loves to cook, but I guess we kinda have to do it for her right now. I used it, it helped my mitral valve tons. I don't know if it'll work for congestive heart failure though, it's worth a try."*

Aaron reassured me and promised to keep me updated. I got

off the phone and cried. Strangers ripped open my mom's heart. The heartbeat I listened to inside her womb. It was the heartbeat that I heard when I was sick and laid on her chest. That heartbeat was now in someone else's hands.

I needed more wine and more dancing. So I got more wine and did more dancing. I video recorded and watched our butterflies-to-be, grow exponentially. The next chance I got, I sent my mom a DVD copy of my dance "Red Ribbons", I wanted her to see it. There was so much for me to share with her and I felt there was so little time that we had together in life.

September 25, Aaron called me around dinner time and said that the tests came back. "It's cancer. Mom has cancer..."

My/our mom has cancer. My hands clasped around the phone tighter. "Did you just say she has cancer?"

"Yes. The fluid they drained from her heart showed she has cancer. We don't know where else it is or if the heart is where it originated from." He said very articulately and slowly without emotion.

"Okay. They're one hundred percent sure?"

"Yes."

"It's stage four." He told me matter-of-factly. He was a rock.

The phone then almost dropped out of my hand. I didn't know if the treatment I had undergone would work for her. Stage four usually means imminent death. However, cancer doesn't always have to be a death sentence. The "warrior" in me rose up again. This time it was to fight for my mother's life—somehow.

"Wait—this can't be right. She was fine and then had heart surgery for heart failure and now she has stage four cancer. What happened? I don't understand. Something has to be wrong somewhere—it doesn't make any sense at all." I was so confused and I was not accepting what I was hearing. I was handling the heart disease, even the news about cancer, but stage four, I was not going to accept that. "She needs a second opinion because that doesn't seem right."

However, it was one hundred percent correct. Mom had stage four cancer and a few more tests showed that it was all over her body. The origination site was undetermined at that time. More tests would be needed and then a plan of treatment would ensue.

"Okay. How can I help? I need to do something. I can't just wait around and let this kill her. I do a lot of work for the American Cancer Society, let me start with that. Does she have insurance?

Aaron sighed, "Not yet. She should have it in a couple of months."

We both knew she didn't have time to wait. We had to act now. I got off the phone and got to work on getting mom insurance coverage. I worked until 5:00 pm. There was nothing more I could do that day. Wasn't sure what else to do or say to anyone. I thought a lot about this life. Mortality. Purpose. God. My brother's words "It's cancer." The echo was fierce and unrelenting. I had to escape a bit and walked to the caterpillars.

They had now enveloped themselves inside their silken chrysalises. I stared at them, they were motionless. Every once in a while they would vibrate. This was their way of warding off predators. Nature was a curious and amazing force that it would develop a safety mechanism for all creatures. How would Mother Nature know to do this? It wasn't happenstance, chance or luck. It's all very complex to think about. They were another creature a few days ago and now they were going to cross over into completely changed beings.

Things were moving fast in all areas of my life. I took strong notice of the uncanny parallels with the butterflies-to-be, the timing of their arrival, and the onset of my purchasing them when I did. I had no knowledge of my mom's illness and according to everyone else, neither did she.

I sat on the couch and stared out the window and gazed at the college across the way. I should have been thinking about my mom, but my heart was heavy for another, hoping she was all right. Even though our relationship was strained and left in an emotional "pending" folder, I worried about losing her too. She was close to my mom's age.

All the intricacies and notions swirled in my mind. I wanted to shut it down but couldn't. This was my impossible reality. For the first time, I couldn't figure out how to take this negative about my mom and turn it into a positive. I had to find a positive somewhere but it escaped me. I fell asleep on the couch.

A couple days passed and the news only compounded. Mom was given 3-6 months to live. I wrote a Facebook note:

September 29, 2012 **"3 to 6 months" (not one of my better structured essays but I'm under duress & letting it out)**

"Turn, turn, turn...there is a season...and a purpose for everything under heaven..." I can't dance enough to take my sorrow away. I cannot speak enough to God to pray. I'm not functioning all that well and want to be able to change things, but I CAN'T. I'm HELPLESS...

At this point I do not see the purpose for why my mother has to die so young. The way things are set up in the circle of life: the elders die and leave the path behind for the younger generations to follow...but what was not intended was for the elders to die before their time nor was losing one's child before they've had a chance to live. Things are so wrong and backwards in life. The unjust get rewarded while the just get harmed...it's all backwards. A great misunderstanding is that because I'm a Christian, I'm at peace with all of this stuff AND...that I'm comfortable with death knowing where people go after this life...well I'm NOT at ease with any of this. I don't think anyone handles death too well...I certainly don't.

I had to tell my dad today that the wife of his youth has terminal cancer. I think having to tell him broke my heart more than my first hearing the news from my brother. This is backwards...everything is backwards. I can't help but ask: what were the decisions and curve balls in life that brought us all to this point? How did we get here?

I still never told my mom the truth about red ribbons (she still hasn't seen it)...my red ribbons--a commonality I wished we didn't have...she never saw me dance except maybe a ballet recital when I was 4. I guess I shall remedy all of this soon then...no better time than the present. Although if I can, I will strap her soul to the earth so she doesn't leave. I'm going to have too many questions to ask her 2 years from now. I'm still working on making a baby--the odds are against me. I know I'm going to need a hug several times in years to come from her and there won't be any. I'm going to need someone to love me like Nana did and neither of them will be there. I had too much take my mom away from me and now this--this is backwards.

Then I think maybe in a few weeks I'll stop struggling and stop trying to figure out the "why" and just accept, or will my depression worsen?

My ultimate fear is my cancer returning yet again, as if I had lied about it--is there enough proof now? All the women in my direct blood line attacked and taken, shall that be enough proof to testify on my behalf? There are my tests too.

And as I fall on my knees and ask fervently: "how did we get here?" Did my mom know that her life was half over when she was in her late 20s? Sobering notion, yes? How many 20-something year olds will read this note? Kinda puts a proper perspective on your life. I can say that it's also strengthening me! I'm losing the last I have left to lose and when faced with that it emboldens me. Watch and see the fierce lioness instilled within me. Too many have been pushing my buttons and using me--pushing back comes easy these past days.

Turn, turn, turn...

But she is not gone---not yet, this is backwards. God, if it'd be your will spare her life 15 more years. Yes, I ask boldly before your throne. Have mercy. Two weeks ago life was different, it wasn't this way...what happened. The wind we do not see but we feel it caress our cheeks. Gravity we do not see but we feel the effects as it plants our feet firmly to the earth. God also invisible. We do not see Him but we see how He changes people's lives – trusting in the invisible.

September 30, I spoke with my mom on the phone. I finally got through to her. She could only stay on for a couple minutes.

"Mom, don't worry, it'll be okay."

"It always is." She slurred.

With that , she and I hung up. She needed her rest and I needed to go to work and teach my babies their ballet classes.

October 1, two butterflies emerged from their shells. They must have had their exodus while we were asleep, but this change didn't happen overnight, but their birthing did. It would only seem as if they changed overnight.

A butterfly has its wings while inside the chrysalis. It is growing and changing while we are waiting anxiously for it to emerge. In many species you can see its vibrant colors through a transparent cocoon and catch of glimpse of what it will become. In this case I couldn't see the transformation occurring inside. Their covering was opaque. I had to trust in what I did know about them to come to fruition.

What is seen on the outside does not always reflect what's happening inside. If you're fortunate, you can catch glimpses of HOPE through life's transparent moments.

We were not disappointed to have waited. They were magnificent. They fluttered their wings and flitted around their mesh habitats. With that, I had hoped that mom could be saved somehow.

October 3, my brother called me, "You better get down here quick. Mom's not doing well." My heart dropped.

October 5, my entire family went to see mom. My brother from San Diego, my men-folk and I from L.A., and my other brother, aunt, and uncle lived in Vegas. Her supportive and wonderful boyfriend was by her side and tended to her at all times. He loved mom dearly. It made my heart joyous to know how much mom was loved by this man; and we loved him in return.

None of us from L.A. knew how we would find mom. My other family members had already seen her. My brother saw us pull up to mom's townhome in our SUV and he approached us. He said for only me to go in first because we didn't want to overwhelm mom. I agreed. It was also good that our son didn't see his "Mema" like this right away. We decided to do this slowly and lovingly.

Mom and her boyfriend bought a two story townhome in east Las Vegas. Coincidentally, her sister, my aunt, had owned one in the same complex a few streets over. It was the same model but different home. I remembered the floor plan from my teenage years; I would know where the bathroom, kitchen and bedrooms would be. It's a very odd feeling to have familiarity like that and be in a different place.

The front courtyard had mom's signature welcome décor, mat, plants, yep, this was her home. She loved the macabre, the dark sinister side of horror films, vampires and monsters. It had always confused me a bit because she was truly a gentle woman who loved pretty things and had an incredible gift of hospitality. Dark horror and frills seemed to contradict one another but mom somehow pulled it off. It could be where I get my affinity for a gothic but elegant look in my dance pieces.

My brother braced me for what I was about to see, he entered first. I hesitated, then I followed him. My eyesight was poor at that time, but much better than it is now. Just as my brother said it would be like: hospital bed, rubber tubing for the breathing mask, mom slumped over, looking very tired. He also added that it was hard to understand her.

Mom was sitting upright which was progress for her recovering from heart surgery. She was slumped over finishing a breathing treatment. She couldn't straighten up because of the surgical cut into her chest. I swallowed hard and choked back the tears as I bent down beside her. Her face wasn't as I remembered it. I recognized her, still beautiful but cancer was fiercely deteriorating and encroaching upon her. Cancer is cruel. I hugged and kissed her. I rested my head on her lap. Her legs and skin was supple. How could this woman be dying I thought. Her muscles were still tone, I could feel it and her pulse vibrant, I could hear it.

She asked how I was doing. I chuckled because I was comparatively fine. She said I looked good. I instinctually rubbed her back the way she did to me when I was a child. It soothed her. She let me know by nodding her head.

"You couldn't come visit me?" She was upset.

Ugh, not a guilt trip now mom, please, I thought to myself. The answer was "no". I couldn't. I had no idea she was sick. None of us knew. We had no money to fly to Florida and I couldn't take time off from work, I'd get fired. We went hungry some nights as it was and I wasn't going to jeopardize my family. I had to feed my son. After my cancer battle, it was a dire situation for several years. We had nothing and were working to build everything back up. It takes a lot of time. I kept my mouth shut as I reflected back upon another situation when I should've kept my mouth shut.

There is a time to speak, hence the word and meaning in it equating to: "proper timing". This moment was not the proper time at all. What mattered was my mom and not me.

While I was right to speak up, it wasn't the time or place. I flipped it around quickly and told myself, *"What did it matter. Mom was only expressing how she wanted to see me and be with me. That isn't a bad thing."*

I thought all of this but said nothing. Her words acted as a reminder to me that I needed to find ways to do things and not let anything be an excuse. You can do what you set your mind to do…within reason.

"I need a pillow." She said.

I got her a pillow and helped prop her upright. She then asked for me to help her with her sheet. I did.

"How is it you understand what I say and they don't?" Her voice was gravelly but still mom.

"Because we're connected, mom." I honestly didn't have a hard time at all understanding her speech. I could see how it would be hard, but I was that close to her. If I couldn't catch each word, I'd be able to fill in the blanks just by deduction and knowing her so well. I had to do it every day in my life and make adjustments because I lost a lot of my hearing with the severe fever I had at the cancer clinic, just like when I was an infant with a severe fever—hearing loss and damage. The skill of filling in the blanks seemed second nature to me. There was only one other relationship I had where words didn't always need to be spoken to communicate.

A white butterfly flew past the backyard window. It caught my eye as soon as my thought completed. I shook my head perplexed. This butterfly was taking on a new and fuller meaning for me. I watched it fly around mom's backyard, then looked to her, and I found myself gazing at the white flitting blur. With that as a constant reminder of "The b-fly", I showed mom my point shoes and she loved them.

Mom wanted to see the rest of the family. My husband and son were ushered in. I gave them their space and time alone with her. Our son loved his Mema and he spent many hours with her as a baby and young child.

The hours at my mom's home passed. The fresh paint from the back room was barely noticeable as I wandered through her home. I took note of the articulately arranged designs, the downstairs bathroom had a maritime theme to it. She loved her boat and brought some of those memories back with her. The towels matched and were perfectly folded. It was something akin to Better Homes and Gardens.

Mom never miss-stepped when it came to decorating a home. If she only had two nickels to spend, she'd find a way to make it look like a million dollar piece of art. If she only had two stones to rub together, she'd figure out how to cook a five course meal. She was that industrious and determined and that talented. Everything she touched was going to be presented in a lovely fashion. This was why I was looking forward to having her design costumes with me for my dancers.

Her boyfriend shared that they were in the middle of finishing decorating the upstairs when mom got sick. He showed me around some more. There was a blanket nearby that mom was crocheting. It was housed in a standing bin that had butterflies and rose-like flowers printed on the outside. I read a quote imprinted on it, "It takes a long time to grow an old friend." John Leonard. The word FRIEND was also written on it.

More butterflies…mom didn't have a "thing" for butterflies necessarily. The sign of the butterfly followed me no matter where I was. It symbolized transformation and often appeared when I thought about someone specific. Unless it was a sign that these precious souls I knew were angels destined for heaven.

It was time to try to get mom to sit outside and get fresh air. My brother sat mom up on the edge of the bed, swung her legs over and draped her arms around his neck. I have a photo of this sweet moment. He helped her to the wheelchair and her boyfriend wheeled her outside. "Your mom is having a good day today. Right, honey? You haven't been this alert in a while."

As we moved outside I was asked to lower the TV. It sat on a credenza and so was the DVD of my "Red Ribbons" dance. It hadn't been opened yet though. I desperately wanted mom to see it but didn't want to disturb echoing waters. If it was meant for her to see it, to see my story, then she would. I wasn't going to press it.

We sat and talked a while. It was hard to know what to say but it was good. I longed to tell her about what happened to me though. I wanted her to see "Red Ribbons". Discernment said, not this day, we would have another chance, another time. The biggest lie ever to believe is that we have enough time. Could this be real, I thought. Is this how my history is going to play out; that I and my precious brothers would lose our mom at a fairly young age?

Mom had a handy *butterfly* shaped flyswatter on the garden table that we sat at. She still had her reflexes intact. She nailed each pest as it made a nuisance of itself.

"Nice, mom. You're fierce with that."

She shook her head and shrugged her shoulders. More white butterflies visited us.

"Mom, do you usually get butterflies. I lived in Vegas 15 years and I don't remember a seeing a single one."

She shook head, "We don't get many. First time there's so many."

I started to cry unbeknownst to her.

Lunch was on the way. It would be a pizza feast. My family's favorite fun food. I helped set up the table and gathered papers together. They had butterfly logos on it; another butterfly sign. As I was about to disregard it, I read it and saw it was Hospice letterhead. I stopped. That moment coalesced for me the reality that my mom was dying. I don't think anyone had straight out told me she was dying. If they did, it didn't penetrate. My son put his hand on my hand and smiled at me. He understood what was happening to his Mema. I smiled back at him and kissed his forehead. He helped me arrange the lunch table and we ate a great feast of pizza.

I marveled at how my brothers were perfectly twinned in burgundy shirts, my flower printed dress had burgundy roses, mom and I complimented one another with matching black hair bands. She wore a yellow terry housecoat which picked up the yellow daisies printed on my dress. Yellow was her favorite color. We were all on the same wave length.

Then mom said, "This doesn't taste right." We all took note of it. Later my brother told me that the cancer probably spread to her brain already and messing with her taste buds. I agreed. This disease was moving fast. It was about three weeks since she was admitted into the hospital. This didn't make any sense. I wanted to step on the brakes and halt this situation. I couldn't catch up with the events.

It was time to say goodbye and go back to L.A. We all had jobs, classes to take or teach, and other responsibilities. My brothers and I decided that we would alternate weekends to stay overnight and visit mom and help her boyfriend. We were set to make the last 3-6 months of her life the best they could be.

We said our goodbyes. I squeezed my mom tightly and kissed her forehead. It was hard to tear myself from her. We piled into our SUV and drove back to L.A. The wind from the cool desert air was forced through my hair. I longed to connect with my mom deeper and make all things right and cause things to work in our relationship. This was wind chasing. You cannot catch the wind my friends. You can only hope to have it touch and move you to feel something.

Have you ever chased after something, pining madness, capture it and then only to find it didn't fulfill the needs you had. Why didn't chasing after things and then possessing them fill us?

My conclusion: The insatiable beast of desire can never be filled to how we'd like it to be--FACT. It is usually because our fantasies and day dreams of how we "think" it will be when we achieve our goals are much grander in our imaginations than they ever truly turn out to be in reality. We must beat our dreams into the submission of reality.

Let's look at a son who deeply desires for his father to recognize him for the man he is. Yes, he should be loved and admired and cared for by the father but sometimes and often-times that doesn't happen. Let's say that after 20 years the father does come to recognize his son. The father embraces his son, speaks the right words, but the son still feels empty. Why? Because maybe he found out that the respect he thought he'd finally gain wasn't quite what he pictured. He finds out the truth about his father: struggling, suffering and not integral.

The son then finds out that his father needed his approval more than he needed his father's approval. The wind chasing and catching cycle stops. REALIZATION is what stopped it. BUT, let's not get so down and hopeless thinking that there's no cure because this is where the true beauty lays. When the son finally realizes this, the son can now help the father. AND guess what? Because the son finally let go of his ideas/ideals, he found the truth and bridged a huge chasm by being the one to help his father. The wind chasing stops and the two men can be who they were truly destined to be.

I know this story oh too well...it's quite close to my heart as you can see. I attest to this because I've seen the happy and just ending when we stop wind chasing.

October 6, I spoke with my aunt. She and my uncle weren't handling this well. My aunt wanted to fight and save my mom as much as I did and as much as my brothers. We were waiting for more tests and mom was deciding what treatment to get if that was even an option. We were all helpless. All we could do was wait.

Two more of the 6 caterpillars came out of their shells. They were feisty and learned where the exit to their habitat was. I too learned that butterflies are not dumb. They have intelligence and sharp instinct. They are also not as frail as they appear. They are hardy creatures that want to fly. A couple of them learned when we were going to feed them and escaped. We would let them fly freely around our home for a bit before we gathered them up to return them to their habitat.

One of my favorite ones had shriveled wings. He wasn't going to fly like the others, but was just as important. We helped it onto flowers so it could feed itself. This wee one was a mighty one because it had to fight harder than the others. It was joyful to watch them flit around the roses and other flowers in their habitat. I was inspired by their beauty and wrote poems and stories.

"Vibrant were her petals and mighty were her wings..."

There once was a caterpillar sealed in a silken cocoon. It kept trying to break its way through the walls of its chamber, but to no avail could not.

One day Mother Nature spoke to the caterpillar, "What is troubling you so?" The caterpillar pleaded, "I'm trying to get out of this jail cell. I can't stand it in here anymore. I want to be free. Won't you help me?"

Mother Nature softly spoke "But you don't even have wings yet. If I let you out now, you'll fall to the ground and get hurt and may ... even die. You must be patient and wait. It's not time yet."

So the caterpillar waited & waited & it almost felt painful to keep waiting so long. Late in winter, the caterpillar noticed a colorful and delicate cascade on its back. It hadn't seen anything like it before. It assumed these must be its wings. "Mother Nature, I now have wings, can you get me out of here?"

"You are right, those are your wings, but they're only the beginning of what's yet to come." Mother Nature soothed.

"But they seem ready."

"But YOU'RE not ready. Wait." Mother Nature coaxed.

So the caterpillar waited. More & more time passed. Early spring had arrived & the caterpillar noticed that its body had changed greatly. It seemed to be an almost completely different creature. "Is it time now?"

"It is time." Mother Nature replied.

The caterpillar squirmed & shifted about its cocoon & couldn't break free. "Aren't you going to help me?" The caterpillar went unanswered. "I need help."

It seemed like an eternity but eventually the caterpillar broke through its silken jail & was free.

As it flew into the air, it noticed its beautiful wings & soared gracefully. "I'm free!"

"Yes you are." said Mother Nature.

"But why didn't you help me Mother Nature? You watched me struggle & did nothing." The caterpillar questioned.

"If I would've helped you, you never would have turned into a beautiful butterfly. It was the struggle that made you as beautiful as you are."

It is true--butterflies that struggle to get out of their cocoons have broader wing span & are more vibrantly colored. They are hardier than those that are helped out according to a lab experiment.

So the next time you're struggling to break forth out of your cocoon, just know that it's a master plan for you to have brilliant & colorful wings. Be patient & wait for nature to take its course.

These creatures were free. They had no fears, no hang-ups, no ulterior motives except to fly and spread their exquisiteness and the pollen from the roses. Interesting how the symbiosis mandated that they needed one another to spread each other's life essence. It's a form of procreation to keep beauty alive. "Mom…" escaped from my lips. I was witnessing my mother's life-cycle via the butterflies. I asked God to spare her, but if not, keep her close to your bosom. All humanity queries what happens after we pass from this earth. It is a worthy quest.

October 7, I woke up and visited my butterfly friends. I was about to open their habitat and enjoy their company. My husband reminded me not to get attached to them because we had to release them into the world soon. They needed to be freed. Two of them flew to my chest. They grew accustomed to me placing them there. I cupped my hands over them while they walked on me. I loved how their little feet and wings would brush against my skin.

Inside the habitat, one of the Painted Ladies wasn't moving. I reached out and nudged it slightly. It was gone. I had kept it too long.

Throughout the day I kept thinking how strong a lighthouse has to be in the midst of a storm. Its walls are made from stone; like giant "arms" of protection to anyone seeking refuge inside. We are kept safe in the midst of torrential outpouring from nature. It's good to have a pair of arms to run to that are strong like a lighthouse to run to keep you safe. My husband's arms were like this for me and so were our precious son's.

That night, my husband, son, and I went out for dinner and returned home. We were making plans how to schedule the use of our vehicle and which weeks I would be going to Vegas to help my mom. My cell rang, it was my brother. My heart quickened. The last time I felt this way was when my grandmother passed on.

"Hello…" the worry and panic was already in my voice.

"Mom's gone." My brother said.

"No. Are you sure? I thought we had 3-6 months?" I knew he was sure, but I wanted it to mean something else. I wanted it to mean that she was back in the hospital and just gone from her home temporarily.

"Noelle, she's gone." He was very stern and calm. His steadiness and definitiveness almost alarmed me further, but he was a strong man and knew I needed his strength now.

I dropped the phone and screamed "no!" with the loudest and most painful cry as my heart shattered. There would be no more time together, there would be no more birthdays to share, no more late night phone calls, no emails, no more texts, no more anything. It was over. I couldn't cry, I couldn't move, I couldn't breathe. Then I collapsed to the floor wanting to feel its coldness on my cheek. I could hear the earth consume my heartbeat.

My husband picked up the phone and spoke with my brother and my son met me on the floor. He held my hand and cradled me in his arms. My husband did what he could to comfort me, but there was nothing anyone could do to soothe me. He apologized to the neighbors and explained what had happened; everyone heard me scream about half a block away.

So often in life we chase after things that we think mean the world to us: a spouse, a good paying career/job, friendships, status, approval from people, etc... (you can fill in the blank with your own things) and all of this is fine as long as it doesn't become an idol in our hearts--as long as it doesn't become THE most important things to us. There's so much more that life has to offer and if our plumb line isn't based on true values and true love, then we're just chasing after the wind...we will NEVER catch the wind.

Go ahead, try it on the next blustery day. Open up your palm and try to grab it, try to grab that ultimate career, the status; keep building buildings, keep trying to force things to be successful--are you unhappy? I'm not surprised, you may be trying to fill a hole with "things" when it should be filled with love, god and his love. That void cannot be filled/fulfilled with making more money, building more buildings, buying more houses & cars, etc.

Will any of these things love you back? Please do try to coax your Rolls to give you a hug or comfort you when your life comes crashing down. Please do try to have your big expensive house to fill your spirit with joy. What's the matter? Are you not content? Aren't the 6 figures in your bank account enough to make you feel okay? Do you know how many rich people commit suicide?

The trap is that we keep trying to feel okay by doing these things over and over again. Why don't they satiate? Because the heart is a hungry monster if left to itself; to where it makes us not even sure of what we want in life. We just know that we're not okay and we think by trying to get more of what we think we want is the answer. It's all a lie, it's all a facade. These things will NOT make you happy in the long term.

Most often we find that these things give us that "high" for the moment but fade quickly. We need to ground ourselves in what truly matters.

CHAPTER 10

BREATHE

"Roses do cry when their petals are torn."

There is always a pause before the dance begins. Learn to breathe and take time for yourself. Once the dance begins you belong to the audience. Noelle Andressen

Text © Noelle Andressen 2014

Photo © Brendan Bonney 2014

I would now know and face a world without my mom. This thought was ominous with no boundaries or walls. My entire world was pulled from me and I felt alone. I didn't want to feel this way, I needed relief. I wanted her back. I wanted my 3-6 months back. My husband suggested I call some of my close friends to come support me. He had to go to work in a few hours and as for my son, while I appreciated his care, he needed to be comforted too. He just lost his grandmother.

I just wanted to pick up the phone and call her and prove to myself that she's still there. I swam in a cesspool of confusion. Where is my God in all this mess? How do I get through her birthday? How do I get through the Holidays? How do I get through my birthday?

I just wanted a little more time with her...just those few months we were told she had...through my tears I could barely see anything--where is God's hand to reach down and comfort me?

Within 30 minutes, two of my dearest friends rushed over and held me. The tears poured out and I let them love me through my nightmare in the beautiful and deep way that they knew how. They brought over my favorite wine and we drank...a lot. I showed them my butterflies and shared how their life cycles coincided with my mom's. These two women are spiritual sisters that love deeply, they knew what I was going through. I was also slowly losing my mind and they sensed that. They also knew that I was strong and would get through this one breath at a time. They stayed with me for hours.

The rest of this nurturing, love circle of women, held a special feast for me a few days later to help me through this difficult time. There were 11 of us. One we see as an incredible woman and leader with class, elegance, some sass, and incredible beauty inside and out. She has guided and helped many of us ladies through our travesties. She has a special gift to help people find the "shine" and bring it out of each person.

We sat in a love circle after our meal and we all shared heart felt sentiments and meditations. I thought about my mom and if she was alright. I needed to know. I missed her and every time I thought about my reality, panic struck me, my skin went pale, and my head grew dizzy.

An earthy and motherly woman, led a gentle meditation in which we focused on love. Softly she said, "Breathe. Breathe. Breathe." There were those words again. They had another meaning this time and were now attached to my mom's passing.

Upon my exhale, I saw my mom in a white gown. She was moving with power on top of a mahogany mountain with purple hues accenting the crest of the ominous peak. Her hair was long, deep chestnut brown, almost black. She moved her arms across a horizontal plane with strength and precision; she was dancing. Mom didn't dance. She had 13 left feet. I believed she secretly longed to be able to dance and she was. Could it be she was in heaven dancing. Did she open her heart to God and love?

Simultaneously, this motherly woman said exactly what I was seeing. She spoke my vision to the rest of the group precisely. That was all I needed. That was my confirmation that my mom was safe and free. She was in a good place filled with love and hope and she was DANCING!

A lot can happen in 6 weeks.

6 WEEKS is not a lot of time but a lot can happen in that time. I thought saying goodbye and lying to rest my Nana was the

hardest thing for me to do. I was wrong. Writing my mom's obituary was the hardest thing for me to do.

I could still point to the calendar and touch the date 6 weeks ago. It was real, it was tangible...it later turned into something unimaginable. It's still so surreal and unreal. Just as there's only one degree difference between very hot and boiling; that one degree makes a difference as a friend has shared with me recently. One day made a difference. There's also only one breath between life and death. How precious and fragile is every one's hearts: very!

6 WEEKS ago I was also a different person with different ideas for my life. The integrity is still there however I fortified my foundation even stronger in God. I've had to make strong lines with relationships--Life Is Too Short to mess around. An eye opener and wakeup call, this too served its purpose for more fruit in my life.

Tomorrow I will say my final goodbye to my mom at her memorial service. Not looking forward to it, but I have to move forward--NOT moving ON, just forward.

It was interesting to see how people treated me and reacted to my mom's passing. For the most part, I received love and support. Some cowered, some looked at me strangely as if death had never touched anyone around, and some didn't know what to say, but said, "I'm sorry". The ones that turned and ran away from me wounded me almost more than my loss. I was fortunate that most were encouraging and loving. It's beautiful to see people shine and give and love. Their genuine selves broke through. It's strange how death can be a strong catalyst for many things.

In 6 WEEKS, I had a relationship mend, a few fell out, one further strained, a few were tested, and quite a few made stronger. There is truth in death and life in death depending on how one looks at it. Death can be a reflection of life and how we operate in it. The vision I had of my mom dancing on a mountain was no accident. Life does transcend into the supernatural and spiritual world. There is a lot we don't understand.

On October 13, I had a series of dreams that left a residue of regretful confusion. I would wake up on the couch long enough to question my truth: Was my mother gone? If she was, was my mother truly alright? Was she out of pain? Was she safe? Was it all a dream within a dream that I would wake up from at any moment? Maybe I fell asleep on the phone with her?

The alarm from my cell phone gave no room for fantasy as it woke me from my tormented dreams. It played "Here Comes the Sun" by the Beatles. Mom would sing this to me when I was little. She wasn't a singer but it was mom's voice. What I wouldn't give to hear her sing these words to me now: "…It's all right…" It was not a dream, this was the horror I had to learn to face: My world without my mother. A wine bottle was perched on our bamboo coffee table, I'd take a swift sip and fall dizzily back to sleep. I didn't want to feel this way. I wanted relief from my pain and this was a short cut I had to take to keep my sanity.

My commitments were intense and planned months ago. I had two performances and one film shoot approaching, the contracts were solid, I couldn't break out of them. I had no other choice. I had to teach my dance classes, perform, and shoot a film.

Many people were counting on me. I didn't miss a single commitment and I performed better than I and others expected under the conditions. I managed to continue performing both shows for an invitational with a 102 degree fever. My partner helped me through it and to date it was the best performance of that duet we ever did. The only thing I missed was teaching at a master class for this invitational and that was due to this flu that had me bedridden. My doctors and husband said if you get out of bed you will be in the hospital and get everyone sick. It was one of the worst flus that was very contagious. I had to be responsible and be professional. It was advised that I cancel that teaching engagement and did so. The director was very understanding and we set a future "to do promise" date for me to make it up to her.

I kept all my other upcoming commitments except that one (due to severe illness) without misstep to the outside world; however, inside I was drowning in my pain and danced in spite of it. I put all my efforts into my company and blocked out the pain from losing my mother.

As the company continued to grow faster than we all imagined, we found some enemies along the way. When you get to a certain level in your career in any business you graduate from being the up-and-coming darling whom they build up and are then seen as competition—a threat and are torn down or at least they tried to. However, they did whatever to prove to others this wasn't happening to save their "face"; very manipulative and cruel.

Not to give the wrong idea because most were incredibly supportive and secure in their talents and achievements and never tried to pull us down and use dirty tactics against us (dirty tactics isn't healthy competition, it's cowardice). I also deeply loved the dance community and that was seen in the fruit of my labor as I've always supported all artists, assisted at other's shows, gave stipends, treated them well, etc. Only a very small handful reminded my board and I of the films "Heathers" or "Mean Girls", as they wrung their hands waiting for me to falter. We were warned about this group and to steer clear. We did. However, they went after us. It was a ridiculous notion to see some in their youth (which is excusable to a point due to "in"-experience) and some were mature adults (which is inexcusable due to experience) leading by this poor example of insecurity and passive aggressiveness.

They began supporting those around me, helping only them and attempting to push us in a direction "they" wanted us to go in. They never had kind or encouraging words for me. Even if I assured them that when you compliment somebody and support them, it makes you look good, not bad. It doesn't detract from your beauty, art or whatever you do. They then said, "okay" and did all these lovely things for others but not me. I had to laugh with my son. He said they were jelly. I used to think that jelly was something you put on peanut butter and bread. My son informed me that it meant jealous. It was high school days all over again.

My board found out that we were kept out of performances; the flu that I had turned into a rumored exaggeration as to why I missed "ONE" commitment; they gossiped about me not "being human" because I was so nice and happy (it is what people of faith are supposed to be like and then if I wasn't nice one time I was a bitch—I couldn't win because they didn't want me to win); they took my copyrighted words and videos off social media and claimed them as their own. One was so obsessed with me they spoke my words in speeches and re-posted them as their own words (almost like a plagiarism secret code to show their allegiance to the small, petty group). It seemed strange why anyone would want to copy someone else because it pegs them as un-original. Being inspired by someone or something is completely different.

Once someone said my own words back to me and a board member overheard it and immediately called them out in public. It solved the problem for it never happened again. My board didn't mess around and was/is quick to deal with things.

The reason for this is one dancer came into my company for 6 months and drove a wedge between me and one of my dearest friends that I knew for years and tried blaming it on me. They also shared our marketing ideas with another director. Now we have confidentiality clauses called in jest our "No-Diva No-Spies Contracts". We also never share anything unless needed. This type of incident never happened again. Sometimes you have make people respect you and your boundaries.

Other annoyances we had to deal with ranged from me being told to stop dancing and accused of being prideful because I had strong confidence in my abilities. They'd stalk my social sites and wait to see who I befriended or who befriended me and solicited them (there's an unspoken social networking rule to not do that and plus Facebook warns against doing this); they used me for my connections and contacts; they'd send moles to my classes to watch me; collect our audience's email information and share amongst themselves; my husband saw one of these mean girls pull my arm in the dimly lit space and drag me over to the light-switches so I could help them. I don't mind helping but doing that to a legally blind person is asking for a lawsuit plus how dehumanizing is that? No one should treat anyone this way.

The most childish of all was if they were connected to another producer whom we just met they would say horrible things about us and tear us down before we ever established the relationship. *(And I was the prideful one?)* We since figured out how to prevent this hideous act from happening again. Some would go after my close relationships and try to get them to not support us. IF that was the case and we were betrayed by the relationship and they took the "bribe/bait", then our enemies did a good deed for us inadvertently and saved us grief by weeding them out—good riddance. There is no loyalty if the base gave way. We always found out who it was.

The worst was a stalker which will be further mentioned in another book and also someone who tore into me so deeply on line. It came from the least expected place. I had posted, "Do you know what has survived all this time through the hardships?"

Someone said "my love"; which was what I was trying to get at. I wanted to make a point in that I never gave up loving after being treated like crap. I was about to boast in HOPE's ability to keep me on the path.

Another said, "Your vanity." I laughed it off at first.

Then I felt dirty inside like I was just attacked. It's because I was. A comment was made about the photos that I shared publicly being an act of vanity. I posted a lot of professional photos on my social media of me dancing but few selfies, and immediately I felt that false guilt (again related to the abuse I suffered). I didn't post my photos because I thought I was gorgeous, I don't think I am, I am awkward looking. Many people told me that they received encouragement by looking at them. They liked it so I shared them. Part of my job as a dancer in the public eye is to be more public with my artistry. It's normal.

Good lord, dozens of times I had been on camera without makeup, hair in shambles, in my pj's, or in garish makeup on stage performing. This remark hurt because I seriously risked so much to love many. I felt like my loving people was the best part of me and one thing that I didn't screw up. I grew a thick skin and told them to shut up and some to their faces. They left me alone and I could not care less any more. I do what I do.

Plus, any time I'd share my dancer's photos they'd have a significant other not appreciate it or they would leave the company by the time we did get new photo, then there's no point promoting someone who was no longer with us, or sometimes we just didn't have their permission.

As time went on, I later found out this person actually wanted to "be" with me and a few months later insulted my husband as an "old bag" that I was lying next to. It gave a heads up to a lustful crush. Another incident was with one who fessed up guilt in an email to me and had the nerve to try to pin the blame and fault on me for having feelings for me. I basically said I have done nothing to lead you on, barely know you, and seldom talk with you. You change your heart's ways or keep it to yourself, I'm married.

Something I had to learn: The way rotten people treated me was not a reflection of me. It was a reflection of them. I say this to you now in case you are dealing with rotten "Mean Girls". Don't cower—give it back to 'em.

This was just some of the despicable things people would do. A plethora of events that are chronicled in my journals could fill volumes of books with their deeds. My response: I loved on them more and gave more and when needed they were called out. This is why I earned the name "dance warrior". I fought this battle with a rose in my hand and love in my heart and that made all the difference. Stand up – Speak up – Don't give up!

I learned that speaking "I love you" or "I forgive you" to your enemies is the heaviest weight they'll ever bear. If they've done wrong, their conscience will eat at them until they make it right no matter what they do. Humility is chalky, bland and hard to swallow at times.

One even yelled at me, "You love me?" No doubt their guilt weighed heavy on them for they truly knew of the horrible deeds they had done. Be careful beloveds, the stains of wrong doing don't wash off so quickly. Oh the weight of the poor soul who goes to bed with a guilty conscience. A clear conscience rests easy and the guilty will feel guilty. Be encouraged that all is not lost.

The irony was found in that these same people would call me up and say the worst things about each other to me. The only loyalties they served were selfishness and betrayal and turned on one another in an instant. Eventually I had to speak up and say that I actually liked that person they were maligning against and would stop chatting. The tearing down of a person is an ugly thing to listen to and I couldn't condone it. This isn't including when you have to hold someone to account for stealing, cheating, etc. These things you must talk about and is not considered tearing one down.

There's a difference between venting and destroying. There's a heart's intent: one is trying to solve problems (benign heart intent), the other causes problems (malignant heart intent). Just look at the outcomes of things and you'll see what the fruit bears. Always do I ask myself: Would I want what I'm about to do done to me? If I answered NO, then I have my answer of how to proceed. What mischief minded people don't understand that the very way they treated me or others of like would be done to them ten-fold by another party. Karma is interesting.

One time my board had actual due cause and proof of wrong doing to our company. A couple years ago, one of these people said they wouldn't believe us until proof was provided so the board provided proof. The board said that it is neither relevant nor necessary for them to believe because the events still occurred. Then the blame was shifted on us. Why? Because, well Nana would put it this way, "The victim of circumstance's body laid strewn on the ground. "Move on." said the murderer, "you're making me look bad."

Meanwhile, I would volunteer for free at their events and shows; I attended their shows and supported them; I wrote good reviews on social media about them and gave free plugs on our company's social media; I donated funds and items like TVs and clothing when they had fundraisers and auctions; I encouraged them; produced them at our festivals; there was so much more we did for these people who stabbed us in the back. I say "we" because it was my board and I who dug in deep and helped. We loved our dance community and all the other communities "THAT MUCH!" It wasn't about us or me. I gave out of my need and went hungry often to bring about the productions we did. No grants except for one time my mentor gave me a space grant. That is a dance warrior. That is a love warrior. That is a light in darkness.

Dale Carnegie set the example of how to treat people in

business and we followed. The thing is, this only works with people who believe in ethics. I deeply loved these people and still do. However, when you give a gift to a fool, he won't know what to do with it.

It was such odd behavior from grown adults. Did they actually know what they were doing? Most of these people we didn't even know or had little contact with so it wasn't because we did anything wrong or hurtful. At times we had to hold them to account and say this is wrong, here's why and here's the factual proof. That always works…unless they're insane.

If you are around people like this—Get away from them, they are toxic. Gas-lighting is seldom an effective tool to use on anyone. People's false assumptions that nice equated to stupidity revealed hearts.

Even though I had tender heart-strings, I was not an instrument in which to be "played". I'm a human being; and when plucked--it hurts. Roses do cry when their petals are torn but it's only that soft revving before the heart engages into action. Some people unfortunately had to learn the hard way: "I can be a sweetheart (rose), however, if you don't want to be stuck by thorns don't pick at my petals. Touch a rose too many times you figure out you're only supposed to look at it, not mess with it. It's a thorn thing."

So I say this to my fellow roses: "Do not under any circumstances make yourself less, feel less, or be less to make anyone else feel better about themselves. Do you realize how strong one has to be to get to the end of a difficult journey?

I implore you to gird up your strength and be that warrior you are.

Loving your enemies produces resiliency. That is exactly what those who don't love fail to understand, you can't undo a loving person. Throwing stones may hurt and wound but it only makes them stronger and tests them to love deeper. The chasm of hate is bridged with LOVE and when one doesn't seek revenge and forgives, they will successfully reach the other side of this chasm to lend a helping hand. The wounding will fade away. Those who throw stones at you once had stones thrown at them. End the cycle. Roses, can you love someone who's thrown stones at you? Butterflies, can you forgive someone who's damaged your wings? Try it. I have. It tested me beyond belief, but I promise the reward is great.

I was realizing more and more that I had enemies. Enough became enough. My board was fed up with it. They said the remedy was simple: drop them. They weren't meant to go where we were heading. We all have our own special paths to pave and theirs running along with mine had run out. My load got much lighter and we found the right people to surround ourselves with. Real freedom comes when you don't give a damn what people think about you. There was much work left for us to do and no time to wade in wasteful things. Onward and Forward.

The loss of my mom caused me to dwell and explore further inward, tunneling inside cavernous enclaves of despair. Where would this path lead me? I groaned heavily like a mother about to give birth, except this was not going to bear fruit of a precious newborn. The "life" coming forth would take on an essence of fear and regret and the birth would be the knowledge that things would be left undone, unsaid, unresolved. She never saw "RED RIBBONS". She would never know that the same hands that exploited her also shattered me. This too would be my reality.

During this time I often wrote journal-like essays on my Facebook timeline to express my hurt in hopes that it would relieve the throbbing of my loss. I also secretly hoped the butterfly would somehow search my profile and read it too. I included a few of those entries that weren't written with grammar in mind, only emotion. This entry I wrote only days after my mother's death:

October 13, 2012

<u>Vision Quest</u>

I need a soft place to fall and someone to carry me because I can't even dance too well right now. I know my feet will find the earth & its rhythm comforting again somehow...it will beckon me to move and create...but first I must find you again, I must know that you're all right...I'm on a quest to know, to see, to hear SOMETHING...I close my eyes to feel the deep pangs of my discomforted breath. If only I truly could breathe, for now it is an illusion and force of will. Wait what was that...was that God's hand touching my shoulder telling me that you're all right? No, it couldn't be or could it really be You. I sense your presence...and for a moment a trickling of HOPE... I breathe deeper and my vision is clearer... I see long, dark, luscious hair swirling in the waves of the wind I see strong arms and movement. I see a mountain: purple, mahogany, and taupe. I see a white garment that adorns your strong body- it billows around your feet...and for a moment my mother was there...I see but not with my eyes for they are filled with doubt, it is my soul that sees you. I'm taken back to embryo and I feel the warmth inside your womb. I'm aware of your sorrows. I'm aware of your pain. I'm aware that you escaped. For a moment I understood your fear (they should have been loving hands, but you were betrayed--I too would know those hands of betrayal--the same hands that harmed you, harmed me.) A message from you for me: strength, love, peace, HOPE. Then a confirmation from you for me: do NOT GIVE UP. Be strong and let your feet guide you, let light be your guide in darkness. Could the end of my quest be near? Could the LOVE that comes from the HEART that overflows with LOVE have reached you. If I had one chance to tell you something--to speak to your HEART once and for all.

October 10, 2012
...and a time for every purpose under heaven...one last time to lay my weary head upon her lap, one last kiss, one last hug, one last i love you, one last goodbye. This was the last photo I took with my mom.

October 24, 2012
The Eternal Siren's Call
Trickling and drifting forward as if we were all masters of uncertainty. Pining for our ultimatum at the crest of life's shore.

Where we may find our resolution to the reticulation of synaptic calls. Oh but if we truly were to understand the cells of humanity.

As light's blinding swell of sacrifice—a love gift with no preceding debt. Chosen by predestination the sojourn in which to alight. Take heed to the beckoning whisper easily overlooked. Unconsciously subconscious do our goals fly adrift. Time stands still for no one.

December   22,   2012

<u>...and then there were ten...</u>

Mom and I most often spent our birthdays together. I did some math, and you know how it is with me and numbers so this may be a bit off, but it seems that there were only 12 birthdays we didn't spend together. That's not too many missed, but looking back now—they were opportunities loving each other that were missed. I'm counting on the good Lord to satiate this with His comfort.

That makes my mom and my nana gone leaving us with 10 in the immediate family.

I went through a lot of our photos together today and I can see how your physical beauty was never tarnished. You were always and will always be a beautiful woman. I can also see the underlying sorrow, which is something apparently I've inherited from you according to people's input. I guess we do have a few woes to not feel completely joyous over. Then there's the other side: the hopeful innocence that resonates through the sorrow. This makes for an interesting dichotomy and causes people to draw near us to investigate; at least that's what it has always seemed to me for as long as I've been alive and aware of this.

Went through mom's things for the past few weeks. I just took a bunch of stuff that was handed to me at her funeral, didn't go through all of it. I suspect my brothers also have more to delve into. So here it is, mom's birthday and I saved the last box purposefully for this day to be opened.

Ah yeah...the last box. I had purposely saved it for today to go through. I had no idea what was in it and when I was in Vegas my aunt Diane, her sister had me "take it"--it was something I wasn't supposed to not take back home with me. I didn't want to open it there so I saved it for today: Mom's birthday as sort of a birthday present to honor her. So I found out why I was supposed to take this box: it had all my baby stuff: a lock of my curls, diaper pins, my baby teeth, pacifier (that's the thing with the black rubber tip bottom left--it was kind of icky but ya know it meant a lot to mom), and my baby rosary beads, very sweet. But there was another box inside that box...

so I found out what was in this little box: a red ribbon, patron saints on charms, and safety pins...a key to my past actually, or perhaps a further explanation to my past and what happened. You all know my red ribbons story...I'm speechless about this...I think I better think it out again...

...and then this...

> *Shirley Gitlin*
> 6-19-02
>
> To Noelle, Bruce, Aaron —
> my wonderful children —
>
> If you guys are reading this, I must be gone — I am expecting to die before any of you —
>
> First of all — no mother could be prouder of her kids than I. I love you all so much.
>
> The junk in these boxes are things I wanted to save — they represent parts of my life. Go thru them, laugh, cry, then say good-bye to me & toss the

NOTE: I received permission from my brothers to share this with you. Thank you Aaron & Bruce! The three of us are giving this to you as a gift. We all love each other and our mother deeply. Please appreciate it as we three share it with you to perhaps help you understand or encourage you in your situation. We all theorize if she knew or not that she had cancer. Did she choose to live on a boat because it was her dream and wanted to live life to the best that she could with the time she had left? Possible. But why not fight? Maybe she was done? I can relate to that feeling.

> *Shirley Gitlin*
>
> junk you don't want to keep. I'm not trying to be weird but I don't want you mourning me. I have had a great life so far & the next few years should be an experience to remember.
>
> Well, enough bullshit!
>
> Love Ya!!
>
> Mom

What the hell does this mean? she told us all that she didn't know about the cancer until she was hospitalized. but I'm reflecting when i went into the cancer clinic in another country for my first treatment...she was drunk and she said something interesting things to me and in light of all of this note: I'm wondering if she's had cancer all this time? i mean, truly, she could've been saying that she was expecting to die before all of us because she was older than all of us and that would just make chronological sense. uuugggbbbb instead of finding answers i found more questions...I'm so confused right now...

my brother said that she asked him about what he believed re: life after death. He's a Christian as I am so you guys know where we stand. She knew where I stood so it'd be pointless her asking me again. I missed this visit she had to my brother's for my niece's birthday celebration. We were supposed to go on a day cruise and have a ton of fun, however, this was training day for me at the new dance studio I was hired at so I couldn't go. Gosh, I wish I could've changed things, but I didn't know she'd be gone 7 weeks later...

I have a lot of questions now. It sounds like she kind of knew that she had cancer...but she swore that she didn't know...

2002: the year she bought the boat with Jim and moved to Florida. She had given all of us some things and she had donated a lot to charity. It seemed odd but she said she bought a boat and had to downsize. Made sense to me.

...and she signs off with the words bull shit...okay mom what were you thinking/doing?

but wait, my aunt saw the CT scan and it was clear last year...so she couldn't have known she had cancer...unless the scan missed something? i don't know what to think.

January 3, 2012

<u>*...and thus i dance...*</u>
to break free from earth's gravity and propel on the wings of angels...
{oh glorious flight}
to breathe freedom from a tightened soul of travesty's past...{by might}
to understand the spirit's cry to express the unchained desires of movement..{a daily delight}
like a siren's enchanted beckoning to the ocean's depths so my dance calls to me...it calls to me but i am not lost to it, for my path is illuminated by the light...{humbly in song}

unabashedly do i offer praise to my lord and savior with my entire being... and thus I dance.

January 5, 2013

My head hurts ~ taking a bit of a break from this virtual word, just needing space between this—this place where I've chosen to lay my crap and my real world—the place where I choose to not let my crap invade...the soft place to fall...I write my "t"s like her...

December 22, 2013

I've concluded after a year of pondering...it doesn't matter whether she knew or not, doesn't change our reality. We just got served an eviction notice – GREAT!

January 23, 2013

<u>*is it really a time bomb waiting to explode*</u>
In the midst of all the excitement and things to divert my attention from so much loss, I forgot that I have something to be grateful for: My 7th year Anniversary of surviving breast cancer round one!

I'm saddened that my mom isn't around to celebrate with me but I'm very glad that I can have a celebration. With all the prep for my show and then getting the flu, I'd almost let my anniversary slip by me unnoticed and unappreciated. I do still struggle with the awaiting time bomb...when will it go off again (because indeed it has)...will I succumb to it or will my body triumph yet again? It's totally not up to me, I get that, my days are numbered like everyone's as it's appointed for us all when we will pass from this world to the next.

Now that it is quite established that cancer runs in my family, especially with the women, I do know that I need to be very very careful of my diet, lifestyle, stress, and all of that. I do still feel insecure about my body and my right breast being smaller than my left, it bothers me still that so much was taken away from me, it bothers me still that people lied about me about my health (this was remedied by showing all my records and shutting them up pretty quickly) but it still hurts at times because it betrayed, it bothers me that I lost my mom so young and then my grandmother only 4 years prior, it bothers me that many turned away from me when I needed them most.

HOWEVER!

What came out of all of that is that many showed their beauty, many helped me recover, many cared, many loved, many gave, and many supported me. I also found an inner strength that went beyond what I thought I could do. I deepened my relationship with God and my family and friends that were true.

I still have a lot of unanswered questions, but am hoping that some answers will return to me soon. (there's more to write...but not quite yet...)

January 28, 2013 ·
I saw her for a moment...
3 a.m. This time has passed by many times since Oct 7th...but it's 3 a.m. today--a random date in time, meaningless even to me, but perhaps not to others.

It's the moments that preceded that pull me from my much needed sleep... I can recall being this sick laying in my mom's lap when I was about 8, she held me and stayed awake until I was asleep.

It was the worst flu outbreak back east and I caught the worst strain. I remember drifting in and out of consciousness, "is she asleep?" My grandmother asked..."Yes, but I think we need to take her to the hospital if her fever doesn't break..." Mom said. That's always the issue: the fever breaking... My autoimmune issues were always a challenge for my health as it was. When I get sick it puts me in further jeopardy. I have to be so careful.

I'm lying on my sofa wishing I had my mom's lap to lie in. She knew *what to do, she always knew what to do. I went to call her today-i had to stop myself and say. "She's not there, Noelle."*

I called my aunt, her sister...she suffers similar autoimmune issues: she has lupus, I think also fibromyalgia, etc...she'll know what to do to help me.

She'll know what to do. She'll know what to do. She'll know what to do. I really need my mom. God heal my broken heart.

January 29, 2013

It's not a surprise to me at all. I'd be surprised if she didn't get it at some point. This is by no means a wish, or a moment of clairvoyance but I know all too well about cancer because my Nana had it, I had it...it was inevitable for her (my mom) to have it eventually. She's young though. I was young too. It is peculiar that we all had it within 7-8 years of one another. We all lived in the same neighborhood in NJ and in Vegas...makes me think a lot about our environment and our predisposition genetically to this disease...

I can't help but think about how close she is to someone else's age...someone who if she were to pass on, I'd be so distraught-never the same again...just as much as if I'd lost my mom. I can't explain it, but it is what it is...truly the things in this life are only put into proper perspective when life itself is threatened. I have such a strong reaction to this notion...and yet I dwell on echoes of words that run deep within me: "Do you hear me? My next question: Do you remember the GOOD???...or are things momentary and fleeting??? If I had the chance to tell you something: I love you..." Would these words if said again to you finally break through? Do you hear me? I truly wonder...I truly do...I'm overwhelmed...I need to go for a walk and pray...I need to pray for many things

January 30, 2013 10:20am
Bruce: I can't even tell you how many times I have had a dream and she's still around just to wake up and face reality. The toughest part is working with Bree through this. She keeps talking about dying and how Ripley and Mema are in heaven.

January 30, 2013 12:5pm
Oh my gosh…yes that's tough…it's hard for the little ones to process, it's hard enough for us big kids. Jared and I were just talking about Ripley. Tell Bree I saw Mema dancing in heaven…oh my she was even more beautiful and strong. Funny, she was never really coordinated lol but I knew she had desire to move and admired dancers…we will all be united someday…the absence does still hurt thought. I guess it's what keeps me not anchored to earth but our final destination. I'll be praying for you guys about this.

No answers – More questions.

During this time to worsen the circumstances, we were facing eviction, this would actually be the second time we received notice. We had no way to pay our bills after working so hard to travel to Vegas to help mom and pay for other things. Things seemed hopeless. I didn't see any signs of "The b-fly", it was a grave situation.

CHAPTER 11
DANCE WARRIOR®
··•♥ ɘ|ᴅ ♥•··

"It is devastating what fear can do to shift our fate and carve out our lives if we let it rule us."

"If the wind had wings to carry the rose, in flight it would fight with valor to defend LOVE and HOPE." Noelle Andressen

Rose Water Choreographed by Jared Kale
Assisted by Noelle Andressen
Title inspired by the film "Rose Water"

Choreography inspired by true events in the author's life.
Photo © Brendan Bonney 2014

And so it went down in my history that I lost my mom at a young age. We, my brothers and I, all lost our mom at a young age. My aunt lost her sister and best friend, my uncle also felt the loss. Mom's boyfriend lost his soul-mate. There was nothing comforting about this loss; it dug deep into our hearts. Right alongside our pain, it'll also be carved in memory's stone that she died well-loved and well cared for.

Her boyfriend, who may as well have been her husband as far as I'm concerned, said that he'd stay until the very end no matter what. He held true to his words. Honorable man--he loved mom so much! I'm grateful she had a man that loved her dearly. She saw all of her loved ones one last time before she left this earth. THAT is a grace from God. There were several opportunities for her to have left this planet but she waited until we came to see her.

From that point on I wouldn't have anyone to turn to about the things that moms are supposed to be there for. There would be no more weekend phone calls, no more questions about high fevers and cramps, no more shared birthday celebrations (our birthdays are only days apart), no more naked baby angel ornament hanging traditions at Christmas time. One angel for each of her own real life babies and grandbabies that I'd hang on her tree most Christmases when we were together.

Mom lived a hard life but a full one. I don't think she had any regrets, but I didn't ask her. She wanted to live on a boat--she did that. She wanted to sky dive--she did that. Anything she wanted to do--she did, except see me dance. She never got to see me dance except for a disastrous ballet recital when I was 3.5-4 years old. I couldn't help but think of a horrible irony and felt guilty again. I survived cancer and danced, my mom died from cancer but was dancing on a mountaintop in (heaven?).

I remembered the blanket she was crocheting. I was going to help her finish it when I went to visit that coming week...that never happened. My brother graciously gave it to me so I could finish it in her honor. I now keep it on my grandmother's rocking chair to remember them both. I spent many sick days wrapped in my mom's love and rocked myself in my grandmother's comfort. Granted it's not the same as flesh and blood holding you, but it's all I had and will have from then on.

I felt alone. I thought I had more time. 3-6 months. What just happened?! I wanted my 3-6 months back.

How does one put the pieces back together once they've been jumbled up and tossed like a stormy ocean of tumultuousness? Carefully, prayerfully, diligently...and yes painfully too...but it must be done.

I didn't feel whole, I didn't feel completely comforted, I felt confused. This was going to be a long process but sharing did help. I fought to not isolate, as isolation has always been my default. Thus far, I'd been able to continue teaching my dance classes, I stayed around other people, I danced the best I could. I missed attending a great deal of my dance classes as a student. I didn't feel safe. My dancing often exposed my heart and at that time I had to protect it.

Mom was going to help me with our first dance festival, "Awakenings & Beginnings Dance Festival 2013 – Los Angeles". She was excited and I wanted her to be a part of it. The message of our video fundraiser changed from helping some young dancers put on a show to a story of my overcoming the hardship of losing my mom. I spoke about how I lost her and that I was keeping her memory alive by honoring her with the festival.

The fundraiser was a success and we were able to produce the show and I emotionally held it and myself together to do my job as the Artistic Director. It was a challenge but we all loved doing it. There would be another time to mourn, but for now I had to pick myself up and be the leader that I had to be. Over 100 people were counting on me to guide them. Going through dress and technical rehearsals took over 15 hours. It was wearing me down. I held it together and kept calm except at one point when I had lost my patience.

As I made my last rounds to check that props were set, set pieces in their proper places off stage, and that the stage crew was ready to go, I double checked an apparatus I was going to dance on. It consisted of several mirrored panels and fragile. I lifted the protective blankets and saw it was now cracked down the middle. I had looked out for everyone, was a gracious hostess, answered everyone's questions and gave others extra time to tech out of my company's tech time. The broken glass pushed me a little too hard. I informed my husband who was the Technical Director for this show and said "fix it". I completely lost it. I ran into the bathroom and turned on the shower and cooled off under the water.

With my clothes still on, I realized what I had done. I had to figure out how to dry my costume in time for the show or use something else. This was a time I needed my mother. She never stressed, and handled things smoothly or her façade was so strong that I couldn't tell if things bothered her. Although it could have been why she drank so much, she may not have handled things well at all but would never give it away.

As I took off my wet costume, my hand ran over my right breast. It felt something hard. I panicked and checked it again. It felt like a lump. Another lump. I shoved it away like an unwanted coat in a dark closet and took a deep breath, turned off the water, dried myself frantically and wrung out my costume. I would have to dance with it wet. It was deep blue. It would be fine. I would be fine, I told myself this as I wiped down the mirror and fixed my makeup.

I looked up and I caught my eyes in the mirror. For a moment I saw my mom. We had the same eyes. My hand reached out and traced the outline of my eyes. It had only been three months since mom's passing. This loss would not heal quickly or easily. There was much work that needed to be done inside. Often I still felt like a sweet, little fairy, crouched on the meadow grounds, holding myself so I wouldn't fall apart. I would not let that happen to myself. I told myself to breathe. I would get through this somehow. The guests were arriving, the house music played in the background and the dancers were knocking on the door. This venue had only two bathrooms.

The show sold out and we had one of our first previews in LA WEEKLY. It's amazing how things can come together in a crisis. The dance community, my mentors, my dancers, my Board, the other companies and dancers were extremely supportive. There was so much love and respect for me to fall back on; however I don't believe any of them knew how much my insides were shattering, shard by shard.

The success of subsequent festivals went ballistic, each show sold out consistently and to this date has had over 50 professional companies perform from Los Angeles, St. Barbara, New York City, Brazil, and everything in between.

We engaged with the dance community from various cities and grew our programs for the festival. We started a children's program, an educational program, workshops and master classes, added more shows, a glamorous VIP Red Carpet Reception, and had a lot of fun. The Board Members for Rubans Rouges Dance shined, our sponsors and supporters advocated for us and it truly unified the dance arts in the community and will continue to do so and grow into the horizon.

Things improved universally for us. My husband's mother and our dear friends from Vegas gave us a loan to pay our back owed rent and we were able to stay in our home. My husband started a great new job that he loved and we were working ourselves into a great position. I was hired on a regular full time instructor at a lovely dance academy and finally, it felt like we had a normal or close to normal life again. I was surrounded by strong women who supported me.

Women are amazing creations. They get the choice to be a mother or not; can choose to be married or not; can wear pants or dresses; multi-task; be soft and strong; balance being a homemaker and a world changer; be a leader and or a follower depending on what helps her and/or the community; her deeds are well known by the mark of her self-confidence and should she not feel confident she humbly states she needs help and support; she loves deeply and with commitment never apologizing for it; give a comforting embrace when she may need it more than someone else; a support for her partner and when all else may fail, her winning smile can cover a multitude of mistakes. Women are amazing.

During this time, another amazing woman was creating an international version of her movement festival. She was expanding to greater reaches and audiences. It was an exciting time for my company and dancers. We went international in a short time, I was so grateful for my mentor working hard on all our behalves to produce this project abroad. She's an amazing lady and can cause "anything" to happen. If she dreams it, she will make it.

We were all excited to tour the areas nearby and see the grand sights of the spired buildings and learn more about the fascinating Turkish culture. It was going to be an adventure. My Board began fundraising for the cost of the trip, rehearsals, and the performance. My mentor was coordinating every detail involved with this artistic expedition. We were all set and ready to perform in Istanbul, and fate would have it that it would be postponed due to no fault of my mentor. It was just not meant to be. It was deeply disappointing but this is always a possibility in every aspect of living life. There would be another time.

We would find out later that we were possibly spared any potential harm as uprisings were occurring after a cease fire. The U.S. Department of State had issued a travel alert: "...The continued potential for terrorist attacks, particularly in the Middle East and North Africa..." However, over 30 million people annually traveled and toured Turkey and for the most part it was considered safe for tourists but with this as a caution shared by USA Today on 1/27/13: "U.S. government employees continue to be subject to travel restrictions in southeastern Turkey. They must obtain advance approval prior to official or unofficial travel to the provinces of Hatay, Kilis, Gaziantep, Sanliurfa, Sirnak, Diyarbakir, Van, Siirt, Mus, Mardin, Batman, Bingol, Tunceli, Hakkari, Bitlis, and Elazig. The Embassy strongly recommends that U.S. citizens avoid areas in close proximity to the Syrian border." Istanbul was not listed. (However as we know now, this lovely city would be attacked in 2016.) Like any city you visit or live in, there are potential risks and life is messy and has the potential to grow into chaos and danger at any time anywhere.

For this particular time, things weren't working out for us to travel to Istanbul. I had learned not to press something that isn't aligning, life and the universe wanted it this way and I had to respect that and let it be. Someday I would love to go visit and perform there. I knew something else would present itself and it would be perfect and suit a need that maybe I didn't realize I needed in my soul.

Not too long after this disappointment, a last-minute light shone through. My same mentor asked how I'd like to go to New York City! It took me about three seconds to say YES! Let's do it. My Board approved and used the money that was raised for the Istanbul trip for this one.

My then duet partner "Angel" was a solid male counterpart for me. We had an intricate and thought-provoking duet that wowed crowds. The weight sharing and balance shifts were mind blowing. One particular lift had such risk to it that one in ten times we would not nail it; and that made it exciting as a performer. This move has since set trends and many have lifted from this and took information from one of my videos on how there's another way to get out of this movement and used it in their choreography. If you search the internet you'll see what I'm speaking of.

When you create good art, others want to be a part of it and often take or copy the original. Then again, there's nothing new under the sun or sunset. I just try to use different colors to make my sky and sunset more vibrant.

I informed my partner of this new project and he was committed to the project. Rehearsals began and the reality that I was going to go back home made me feel ecstatic and also stirred with slight trepidation. I had not been back since I was a youth. I had not seen the place of my suffering in years; but that was a long time ago, surely I had recovered enough emotionally since. I felt I could face my childhood horrors.

With so many last minute changes in plans, flights, and performances, I was getting nervous. I was also not one that liked to fly, still not thrilled with it. My nerves and thoughts of dread controlled me to the point that I would need a lot of wine or Benadryl to knock me out for the ride. After September 11th, I was even more fearful of having my body hurled into the atmosphere with no safety net. It was also a fear of heights issue.

To remedy this fear of mine, my beloved husband and son took me on a few Ferris wheels. This is cruelty. I closed my eyes at the highest points. They took me on every coaster at 6 Flags Magic Mountain and had me repeat X-Treme four times in a row.

Ferris Wheels o' Death are the worst especially when they keep you at the highest point for a few minutes leaving you dangling, unstrapped, swaying to and fro without much protection. *Today I am still afraid of heights. I am still afraid of flying. However, I love lifts and throws and have such trust that my partner will catch me. I don't know what the difference is, but there is one.*

The night before my trip, I almost cancelled my flight to New York City because of my fear. My husband said, "Don't let fear keep you from doing what you want to do. You've come so far. Don't give up now." He was right. I would force myself to go on that "red-eye" flight the next night.

The day of my trip my son and I took a walk around the neighborhood park. He held my hand and told me that I was going to be fine and I was going to have a great time with my dad and family back east. My head hung low and I watched my footsteps carefully step over the protruding mulberry tree roots.

"This is just like when I was a little girl walking home from school." I said as I smiled and as looked up at him, and felt something approaching us. I felt that familiar pull in my heart. It was that pull I felt when I was near…

...and there she was. The butterfly drove past us. I tried not to look obvious that I saw her so I kept my head slightly angled downward but I wanted to see her. I wanted to run up to her or at least wave; but I didn't. I didn't seize the moment, I didn't do any of those things.

"That was her, wasn't it?" I questioned whether I truly saw her or not.

My son nodded, and a yellow swallowtail breezed by. Before I could point to it, it was gone. It was gone just like her. Another missed opportunity, it is devastating what fear can do to shift our fate and carve out our lives if we let it rule us. I felt my chest ache and I condemned myself for being fearful.

My mom's memory also engaged with me that day. The sign of the butterfly had been everywhere. While I talked with my best friend Sheila, I saw 5 Monarchs flitting about. They loved to fly over my head, tease me and beg me to chase them, so I did. I've been called silly for my antics, but seriously, I doubted my mom would share this opinion at this moment. She probably wished she could have chased butterflies with me in the park even with her full life of adventure.

She at that point truly knew one way or another what life should really be about. It's not about competition, or racing to beat someone out of something, or manipulation, or greed, or lust, or material goods. None of those things mattered to her right now, neither did they matter to me either. Only she mattered to me. It's truly all about LOVE. I deeply believe we all find out the TRUTH when we die; but did we need to know the truth before-hand?

My husband and son drove me to LAX to catch my plane. They waited in line with me to enter the airport. Things were vastly changed since I flew last, it was twenty years ago. I watched people take off their shoes and there were giant cylinder x-rays that we had to walk through. I shook my head with disbelief. "Am I really getting on a plane? I haven't seen my dad in years. This is so odd. I'm not going. I'm going to die on this plane." A few people looked at me with disdain when I said that. "It could happen you know."

My husband kissed my forehead and our son squeezed me. I was getting on a plane and living out my dreams while taking this huge step battling my fear of flying, in addition to my fear of heights, and possibly the fear of getting air sick too.

"You're going to be fine. You're going to have a lot of fun with your dad, go see your old stomping ground. You'll come back with stories to tell. You once told me that what you wanted to do in heaven is what you always wanted to do on earth--DANCE. Remember how you were near death in the clinic. You survived all of that and now you're here. You're flying across the country to dance—in New York City."

"Baby, New York is not heaven." He chuckled and kissed my forehead again.

"Breathe." He said with a voice similar as when he told me I'd rise from my sick bed. I still had much yet to do.

I nodded. "Okay, but if I die it's your fault."

"Of course it is." We both laughed as he nudged me to the security gate.

The next thing I did was take off my shoes and handed them over to a stranger for judgment.

Sleep escaped me for most of the flight even with wine. I constantly checked my cell for the time and waited for the sunlight to make an appearance. The guy sitting next to me was a business executive for some kind of financial firm. Every time the plane moved or shifted suddenly I asked him if that was normal. He found my fears amusing. He kept asking if I wanted to have a look outside. I kept saying no because the wing looked like it was going to break off. I had him take a photo outside the window for me instead. Regretfully, I peered outside a couple times only to have vertigo swell about me. I had the stewardess help me to the restroom so I could breathe and splash some water on me. Anxiety attacks are not fun.

The plane landed and I dashed out of it barely hearing my new friends wish me luck on my performance. I had told my brother to meet me at the baggage claim. He asked what my luggage looked like. I told him I didn't have any but my carry-on. I just thought that's where we're supposed to go to meet everyone so that's where I told him to pick me up.

Too many years passed since I saw my father. I couldn't wait to give him a big hug, catch up on old and new things, and speak about mom's passing. He was currently married to a beautiful and wonderful woman who I often saw as a step-mother and friend. She had a great sense of humor, generous, and loyal. Her down-to-earth sensibilities were contrasted with her creative side. I still love her and so glad she's a part of my family.

We drove up the driveway and there he was, very similar to how I remembered him: brawny, handsome, and stealth like. I never saw him smile so broadly. I ran up to him and threw myself into his arms. We were really together and I was back in my home town.

The homes, the buildings, the scenery, were overlapped by visions of my past. It felt like a film projecting onto the real world, intruding and reinterpreting my history.

Dad brought me inside and my brother carried in my carry-on bag. My dad, his wife, and my brother lived in a two family-two story Colonial styled home. This was a magical place with memories on shelves. My other grandmother's hutch, beer steins, picture frames, so many relics from my past.

After I settled in my dad took me for a ride around town. I hadn't seen my grammar school since I was around ten years old so he took me there first. He said it looked radically different, he was right. The only thing that I recalled was the large paved hill the school sat atop that my brother and I used to snow sled down. It was the only thing that looked vaguely the same. For many winters, we found ourselves on that hill that was enchanting and filled with laughter, snow, and we underwear. At that point, we couldn't wait to get home to have our underwear toasted dry on the radiator. Soggy underwear was our signal that it was time to leave our sledding escapades and go home before frost bite bit us.

We then drove past my childhood best friend's home and a grocery store. Flashes from my past nightmares began to steal my present moments; we were getting closer to the home that I lost my innocence in. I looked down at my chest, I could see my heart pulsing and it felt like it was going to break through my skin.

The house where my innocence was shattered loomed in front of me.

"Dad…" My eyes stayed focused on that damned house as we drove by it. It looked exactly the same. I hated that house.

"Do you remember that old house?" He asked me unknowing what his words were doing to me.

I slightly nodded my head. "Yeah." I remembered that old house very well. I remember how my grandfather molested me. Heat from anger rose up inside of me. I stared at it so intently that my gaze could've knocked down that prison which held my memories. It was a painful moment that I didn't want to remember but I wanted to face my demons. The car kept driving past and we pulled away and it faded like the nightmare I had. Perhaps another time; perhaps I would see it again someday.

My dad pointed down the street. "That's where Mozart TV was."

It was an empty lot. It had been torn down. Something happened to me there too. I couldn't or didn't want to remember what it was. I felt a sense of vindication knowing that it was razed to the ground.

He took me past my other childhood home, the one I spent most of my youth in. It looked so small. The driveway looked the same, as did the garage that I hung fabric from to act as my backdrop and curtain. This was my first outdoor auditorium. My Nana and I spent hours dancing, singing and acting in our backyard. I charged the kids on the block a dime to come see me perform, but then I ended up putting them in my show. I never liked performing alone. We then got our parents, older siblings, and other friends to watch us, and we charged them a quarter because we knew that they had the money.

We performed our versions of whatever was the hottest movie trend for that year. We did Star Wars, JAWS (the musical), Grease, and tons of my favorite Broadway musicals; West Side Story was my favorite. I'm certain we were hilarious. Our version of R2D2 was a tin garbage can turned upside down that my brother donned and when we did JAWS, we used an orange inflatable dolphin in our wading pool. My Nana would bring home the playbills from the shows she'd see and teach me the songs and choreography. She knew I was meant to dance and most responsible for keeping that dream alive.

Dad drove us down the turnpike and he pointed to where the Twin Towers used to be. "You never saw The World Trade Center, did you?"

"Mom never wanted me to go to the city when I was little. She took me to see two shows and to the Museum of Natural History and the Planetarium once. I don't think she went there either. Nana did though." If it weren't for my dad, my brother and I never would have seen Watkins Glen, Waverly, Corning, and the Catskills. New York was not just Manhattan.

He told me his account of September 11th and how he saw the second tower come down. It was an iconic pair of what he called teeth "like a saber toothed tiger" that jutted up into the New York city skyline. The eerie part about his account was how close he was in proximity to this national disaster. I had only seen it on TV in Vegas.

I shared with my dad how I felt a strong urge to be close to our son on the eve of 9/11. I told him the accounts of our day on the west coast.

Our son had bunk beds and slept on the bottom bunk. I crept into his room late that night and put the top mattress on the floor next to him. I had no idea what I would wake up to. No one in the world did.

My husband rushed into our son's room and turned on our son's mini TV set. "What's wrong?" The little screen soon revealed to us what was wrong. One of the twin towers had billows of black and gray smoke emerging from it. "It's a fire or something. My partner just called me."

This didn't seem like an ordinary fire. "There's something wrong, it's something else." I said as my husband kissed my head and left early for work. He said he'd call and check in later. I had been working on Ted V. Mikels sequel to his Astro Zombies film as an actress and script supervisor (odd combination), we were shooting later that day. I couldn't call in sick but wanted to.

Our son woke up and sat on my lap. "What's that?"

"Something evil, son." I told him as I hugged him tight. I explained how my dad, his family, and my other relatives and friends lived back there and they were all I could think about. This didn't feel right, there was more going on. I felt it. I must have sensed it the night prior.

The camera angle on TV suddenly switched and a plane burrowed into the second towered. I was stunned. The news was reporting it as an accident. Immediately, I recalled the incident in 1993 at the World Trade Center. This was not an accident. We were under attack.

I was extremely worried about my dad, and all of my family in NYC. I couldn't get through for hours, not even internet was getting through. Finally, I did get through and everyone was all right. Jane was trapped in Newark and had to walk most of the way home. It was a mess and very frightening.

My dad also knew that we were under attack that day. After we exchanged stories of our 9/11 experiences he told me not to go into the city alone. He said he wouldn't be joining me or seeing my performance. While my heart was saddened and disappointed, I completely understood and couldn't blame him. The terrorism and crime concerned him.

After a day of sight-seeing, and re-visiting old places and buildings, his wife made an awesome dinner. We ate on their outdoor deck that overlooked their garden. Gorgeous wild life flew from the trees. The sounds took me back to my childhood once again. The air, scenery, people, was worlds apart from Los Angeles. Not one being better than the other, just different.

We went inside and sat on the couch. My pointe shoes were staring up at me from my bag. I resigned to their pleading and put them on. I warmed up and danced a little bit. It was the eve before my performance.

My dad marveled at how beautiful I looked in my pointe shoes. He also said that he felt that I missed my calling. I asked him how? He told me I was too short and the extra inches that my pointe shoes added made a difference. I laughed, he still didn't realize that his baby girl had not missed anything and was living her dreams, and there was more to follow. Our company's first tour was only the beginning.

He said that I was good and that I had a gift and urged me to make a lot of money at it.

"Most dancers don't make a lot of money dancing. It's hard work and barely pays bills. It's was worth it though. I love my art and I'm not going to give it up this time." I sat on the couch next to him and showed him how I laced up my pointe shoes. He found it fascinating as he squinted through his eye glasses. He asked if it hurt to wear them. I told him yes, but after a few minutes when

I'm dancing it doesn't bother me.

"Do you miss your mom?" He carefully inquired.

I could only nod my head.

"You gotta move on, sweetie. It's been a while. Is it any better?"

"No. It seems like yesterday still. She would've loved all this. She's missing it. I can't let her go." I played with the laces on my pointe shoes. This was an old habit of mine, to play with laces, ties, or my fingers, when I felt anxious or out of control.

So there I was in NYC with my duet partner ready to perform for an audience. We did it and it was flawless. Afterwards, many approached us and shared how it touched them. My dance pieces were resonating with people on both coasts, and everywhere in between. There was something more to this than coincidence. This was my calling. This was what I was ultimately put here on this planet to do but I still had questions. The very thing that was taken away from me, hidden from me, and almost lost to me from the perils of cancer and almost death was what lifted me up. It became a vessel of love and HOPE. I came back home and my life had changed and I was once again different.

My trip home was brief but needed. Saying goodbye to my dad was terribly hard, but my life was in L.A. I missed my son and husband. The comfort of my own bed met my aching body in L.A.

Part of restoring my relationship with my husband was found in the little things we would do for each other. He would randomly but intentionally create songs for me, I would get him cards and write sweet notes, we would help each other with projects or just hold hands and squeeze each other. Love doesn't have to be found in expensive gifts, it is found in the humble acts of kindness. There was a lot of work done and yet to be done in our union but when you have two hearts willing, it makes all the difference.

One of my favorite gifts he gave during this time was a stone. He gave one to me that had the word HOPE inscribed into it. Our son received one from him too that said FAITH. They were the perfect words for us and we kept them close to our hearts. It served as a reminder that something bigger than us was there in the midst of adversity. Heart mending was continuous.

With our NYC success, more performances came, dance roles, modeling jobs, singing, writing, a full spectrum of artistic countenance presented itself along with temptations. Each job that came along I took and excelled, I didn't think twice to turn anything down at that time.

My frailties and strengths as a human being were tested. I once again found myself in the midst of the rich and famous, elite parties, and plenty of anything that I wanted. I did as I pleased without crossing the line of my beliefs. I never stepped on anyone to get anywhere, there are some that would do anything to anyone to get anything. I drew the line at that behavior.

When you sell your soul to the devil, you sell your soul to the devil. It's that simple. Not to sound dramatic, but as I look back, I can see where I lost myself again. It was in the familiar form of vomiting in the women's bathroom or a nearby trashcan, however, it wasn't from fighting for my life from cancer and the ill effects of the treatment. I had become my own enemy. I loved wine and still do. That grew into other beverages. Before I knew it I had gone off and away from my plumb line of truth.

A sobering moment came when a God-serving friend saw me in a bathroom and reached out to me, "I feel I have a warning for you. Not all that glitters is gold." She was telling me that I should not be so eager to take any job or project that comes along. I needed to be mindful of the path God put me on and to stay true to it and not be tempted by "anything".

From the toilet bowl, I picked myself up and grabbed my purse. My HOPE stone slid out. I stopped breathing for a moment. I "had" strayed.

From that night on I worked to get back to my beginnings "again". I did not become an alcoholic, however, I very well could've ended up there had I not had someone who cared about me speak up. (Later on I knew "The b-fly" was worried about me regarding this issue. She dropped many hints during class stating that alcohol can be very damaging and posted articles on line for the class to read. However, I knew she was speaking directly to me out of love. This too will be for another story, another time.)

Time and what we do with it is a more precious commodity than money, only few will ever realize this. "Life doesn't offer receipts so you can't take it back. Choose wisely and spend it well." Were the words my Nana told me that were coming back to remind me with love. This made me contemplate much: The Meaning of Life. After so much success and a few months after my mom's passing, I still had questions in my reflective time. Was I touching any hearts? Was I making a difference for anyone? Had I truly lost my way and gotten caught up in all the "things" of this earth?

First I thought I was to be an actress and pursued it wholly, then a model and had success, a film maker and garnered 3 Emmy nominations, and a singer with a decent body of work. However, dance was my first true love and it would return to me as a surprise visitor later in my life when the world was infatuated only with youth. It enraptured my heart like no other art form. I was best at it. The successes came with the other art forms for me, but they were not my lover.

I decided long ago to build my "home" on a rock--a solid foundation of goodness and morals. I needed to remember this and fall back on it during my trials. I didn't have a choice if I was to survive and move FORWARD (not moving on--but forward. there's a huge difference) without my mom. Moving on lets go; moving forward continues on.

Her death caused me to tumble and fall and then make hard decisions about relationships. I needed to start thinking a little bit more about me and my well-being. I gave too much and it drained me. I was in a place where I needed to receive and I was ready to receive. My true friends would understand and do what is needed. This was the perfect time for "wheat to be separated from the chaff", a bit of culling and discovery.

During the next few weeks of contemplation I teetered back and forth on things. I had moments of clarity vs. moments of confusion and pain, I'd be in complete joy and then despair. It was the normal grief process and I was going to go through it no matter what but without a numbing salve. This needed to happen.

I warned everyone if they saw my tears, to not be afraid, I was just missing my mom. I shared that if they saw me joyful, to not think I'm cold blooded and not "handling it" I was seeking a power higher than myself and at times I would gain the peace that passed all understanding in the midst of my stormy ocean. That higher power could calm the waves, I saw it, lived it, experienced it. It takes humility to turn your life over to an invisible God, trusting in the unseen but always feeling its effects.

Many dreams plagued and enchanted my mind at night. Some dreams were of my mom dancing on her mountain top and briskly grabbing my hand to join her; some were of friends; some of me dancing in front of thousands of people; and then one or two of "The b-fly" I had met a few years ago. By chance (or was it), we would run into each other through the years. I thought about her whenever something wonderful would happen, and I wished she could have been present.

She was in my heart when I was overlooking Manhattan on top of the Empire State Building; performing before 1,200 people; preparing for our dance festival; running errands; laughing at a silly joke that she'd like; in rehearsal for Red Ribbons; or dancing in the rain. She was there with me and a butterfly would consistently visit to stab my heart to prompt me to think of her.

Was dance my ultimate calling or just another stepping stone to what was ahead? I began to question even deeper what my purpose was. Was it to help "The b-fly"? Was it to further my dance mission reaching hearts to give HOPE? Was it that I already accomplished what I set out to do? Was my MISSION complete? Why was God always bringing her to mind? Was it all of the above?

I had to return to my beginning yet again. I had to find out. This one woman held the answers, somehow. A complete stranger, had my answers, perhaps not verbally, but I would see it in her eyes. I saw many things in those eyes until my sight began to fail for me.

During the seasonal changes when all things that are green begin to turn brown, The Rose still love The Butterfly. It's still there buried beneath the decay of the autumn leaves.

"Past hurts and woundings when they surface to the top can be like autumn leaves. They're signs of death, a withering on the vine branches. Something had changed and broken off. It wasn't necessarily a bad thing. It was a sign of life yet to come. Seeing her again with the wispy wintry winds subtly appearing, was a sign of winter on the way and a reminder of what was to come next: a rebirth in spring. This was when roses bloomed and butterflies got their wings. Life grows again. Even though it seemed like a cold dark winter on the way, The Rose always kept in mind the love of spring and the joys of the butterfly."

Three weeks later I enrolled in her class and we saw each other for the first time in a long time. We both had been on incredible journeys separately but not completely apart. As I've shared, she was always with me in my heart no matter where I went. My mom and Nana were also with me in the same way. However, "The b-fly" was not deceased, she was here.

Our smiles were awkward and brief, pregnant with past hurts and unanswered questions for both of us. I believed we were both ready to be in each other's lives again at that time. I needed answers and an unsettled riddle between us solved or resolved. I hoped this would be the time.

CHAPTER 12
CAST YOUR STONE
··•♥ ϑ|ɞ ♥•··

"A light in the community, a dance warrior fighting on behalf of others."

Reaching into what is unknown and making it known. Finding the depths within and expressing outwardly. We must stop to think about what and why we are doing the things we do. What is their cause and effect in this world. Noelle Andressen

Photo © Jared Kale 2015

My mom died in 2012. I fell apart in 2013. I lost my way in 2014. I was put back together in 2015. Nana always told me, "God is in the business of turning tokens of tragedies into symbols of triumph in our lives." (I incidentally had this on my Facebook profile and a church in another country slightly reworded it but please know it was from my grandmother.) I had plenty tokens of tragedy which were remnants of already fragmented hopes. How could I with so many frailties and flaws be used to help others?

August 17, 2015 I heard a TV broadcast: *"If you see a stone somewhere, pick it up and ask yourself that question: What is my stone, what is the gift that only I can do in this world to make it a better place? Then spend the rest of your life trying to throw it well." Spoken by Kathie Lee*

Gifford from "Hoda & Kathie Lee" segment on TODAY

What is your stone? Had I heard her correctly? Indeed I did. This was confirmation for me. The token stone my husband gave to me said HOPE. That word and theme threaded itself throughout my journey. I knew HOPE was my stone and that I was supposed to help people by giving them HOPE through my talents; but where do I cast it?

I recalled my promise I made to what I believed was God in the midst of my cancer journey. "If you save my life I will become a fisher of men for you and reach out and give love and show love. I will fight for wounded souls, broken hearts, and lost sheep to give them HOPE. I will let them know that not all is lost."

I first reached out with dance to my husband, then "The b-fly", and then my fellow students and ultimately an audience. I thought, wait a second there's something to this. There's something here.

This was when the particles and atoms, turned into my reality. I would take my skills (my stone) and cast it before thousands in the form of my dance company to give them HOPE; not only that they can heal but have HOPE in the midst of it all. Just like it was once shown to me in the least likely of places: a dance teacher who wanted nothing to do with God. She was there with me in the beginning after cancer and in my recovery. He used her to save me in a way I never expected because I in turn was used as a vessel of love for her. That is what saved me; I learned to love again. This is still perplexing to me, because I always had an anchor of love in my heart for her that would never go away. It was a thorn that throbbed at times. I've just come to accept it instead of wrestling it to death so that nothing magical remains. It is what it is. This is good.

During the next few months, our relationship was strained still but not to the point of devastation. There was still forgiveness and love there for both of us. There is more detail to share in my tale about Red Ribbons...to be continued...

With my new understanding of what my purpose in life was, I felt empowered to reach out to many communities and create wellness groups under our outreach programs. One was called: Dancers Fighting Cancer. It had many facets to it including: free wellness classes for cancer patients in all stages of treatment and recovery; public speaking; performances; and now this book. All concerned wanted to help make this a successful venture. We gladly did all this by donation, we received nothing for our charity and loved meeting so many lovely people. Our main concern was their well-being and survival.

From there I became Chairperson for the Luminaria Ceremony for the South Valley Relay for Life Event. I have served for five years to date in this position without compensation and I stress this because sometimes I am asked how much I am paid. I do this because I love people and I want to see them well and do well. No other motive. I've often been criticized for my kindness and been questioned about it. This was how I was raised. Plus, why do horrible things to people, what good does that do?

The Luminaria Ceremony was a fully produced 30 minute or 60 minute long presentation (dependent on the location) that honored cancer survivors and those who were no longer with us. Each year it was a different exhibition with various elements that involved luminaries, candles, dance, music, film, poetry readings but most important, it was the heartbeat of the people who needed to express their emotions about the tragedy of this disease.

ROSEWOOD, was a sullen yet inspirational dance trio about Julie, Erika and I and the support system we became for each other in the cancer clinic. Three women, one dream: to live. The dance depicts my personal conquest over the disease while I had become close friends with these ladies. Erika and I were very close since she was my next door neighbor at the clinic. She fought bravely but unfortunately succumbed to her disease. Each step along my way I felt that I would be next.

ROSEWOOD was part of a larger and longer 30 minute dance within the Luminaria Ceremony called "Let This Be My Last Battleground". Intentionally, we borrowed it from the original Star Trek series. It perfectly described my mental outlook with this disease--it encroached upon my life once too often and each time I've said: please let this be the last time. I come at it from a place of strength not weakness but of course I don't want to reprise this journey. You always want it to be your last--one battle that you win once and for all. Cancer does not have to be a death sentence.

In a portion of this piece I re-tell moments of my fight. There was an instance when I was lying on my bed in the clinic, my husband kneeling and praying alongside me and our son holding my hand. I began thrashing my head from side to side. I was so ill.

My kidneys were failing and I had a high fever. My vision was failing me and tunneling. I had no peripheral vision and I was too weak to move. I somehow managed to reach my right arm upwards towards the ceiling and begged for God to take me home. He did not take me home. Instead, I felt a strong, masculine hand traipse down my arm to my hand. It caressed my hand and pressed its thumb into my palm and held me firmly. I let the weight of my arm fall into this peculiar being's hand. It looked like my husband's hand, but it was not. It should be my husband's hand.

The next day I woke up. I was still miraculously alive. I had made it through the night. I asked my husband if he remembered holding my hand. He said no. From where he was kneeling beside my bed, it would've been impossible for him to have held my hand. It left an indelible mark on me and I put it in my dance.

My Emmy nominated husband and composer created an emotional tapestry for us to move to. At the time of creating this dance Kristopher only had the melody and name of this composition, he didn't know that it would be the music for this dance. The music worked very well with our movements. He didn't know the theme for this section was about inner beauty. It's something that myself as a cancer patient had to deal with...how can such an ugly disease bring about any form of beauty. Some say the spiritual and symbolic meaning of ROSEWOOD is beauty.

A remarkable element is that I had choreographed the

movement without music. He gave me the music only two weeks before we had to perform. We had no idea if the music would match the movements. It did. The music he scored fit perfect to the choreography I created. We only had to tweak one minor part.

This dance became a staple in our yearly presentation. This presentation was always a beautiful sentiment about the family, friends and loved ones and simple "Thank You", made it all worthwhile. This is where people began to refer to me as a light in the community, a dance warrior fighting on behalf of others and myself.

My next battle was for my sight. I was diagnosed legally blind with borderline glaucoma. There are various levels and degrees of eyesight loss, mine was severe enough to cause me to rethink many things including my dancing. Those rainbow migraines I had in the past were an indication of problems yet to come.

I met this challenge head on and decided to face it with bravery and balls. I wasn't going to quit. If I quit now, I'd lose all I worked hard for and my enemies would win by my default. Not gonna happen! The sky isn't anyone's limit and neither is the moon.

I am still in the process of making this work for me and I still dance. I don't know what the future holds for me. At the time of writing this, I am in the process of finding out more answers and going through many tests. Hoping for the best, but ready for the worst.

With all of our hard work, good work ethics, and charity, we were able to do many other things. Our being able to produce phenomenal shows that caused the audience to "Feel the Experience"®, gave us opportunities beyond our imaginations. One came in the form of being able to work with the legendary dance photographer: Lois Greenfield.

For a moment take in and recall my mentioning how "The b-fly" had those beautiful Greenfield photos. My life has always been about extremes, both good and bad.

What once was a dream, became a heralding reality that had thrust forward with such unpredictable force. How we got there isn't the important focus. What was and is important is that we got there. My dad, his awesome wife, and my brother embraced us again and had us stay with them back east. Everything was in alignment and absolutely perfect.

There I was, three years later, back in NYC. It was the morning of May 11th, the day before my adventurous photo-shoot with legendary dance photographer, Lois Greenfield. Yes! Lois Greenfield. I shook my head vigorously to attempt to wake myself up from the daze. This was not an illusion, this was my reality.

There were many facets that had to be carefully planned and laced together in order to produce a beautiful work of art that was expressive and marketable. I had complete confidence that both would be achieved, what I was more concerned with was navigation and details. I was recovering from a concussion from an accident; my head was a jumbled mess, more than usual. Keeping it all straight in my mind was an impossible feat at that time.

Jay, my assistant, who has become an integral part of my dance company: Rubans Rouges Dance, traveled with me to New York City. He does everything for me from keeping my life organized to helping me remain calm. Details are his expertise. This particular morning, we had to travel from East Rutherford, New Jersey to NYC to try-on and pick up several gowns at Terani Couture for the photo-shoot the following day. Back east you simply don't just drive and expect to get anywhere in a timely manner—you take multiple forms of transportation.

Having been born and raised in NJ and with family in NY, I had familiarity with some places. However, mix a concussion with legal blindness and you have a great potential for either extremely catastrophic or highly comedic things to happen. Jay made sure the catastrophic didn't happen and guided us perfectly through the streets of the Big Apple and I reluctantly made sure the comedic occurred.

We arrived at Terani Couture and greeted by Helen and a few of the designers in their showroom. (We spent 3 weeks' prior via internet swapping ideas of which designs Lois approved and felt would work for the shoot. My Board's input, and what I needed as a dancer all figured into this art project.) Helen told us to make ourselves at home and look around while she prepared the fitting room. This was the second time my company and I would be collaborating with Terani Couture and their designers.

The showroom was a beautiful white tiled, white walled

look. Furnishings were minimal but upscale contemporary peppered with a few six-foot tall, glazed white, human-morphed, modern-art, mannequins. It wasn't stark and sterile, but clean and elegant. The walls were lined with their latest couture. I was surrounded by beauty and I reveled in it. The textures of their designs varied from sleek satins, intricate beading and appliques, mesh inserts and meticulous details. I even got a sneak peek at their next season's in-the-works line. Without revealing too much, I can say that it'll greatly please and be a grander presentation.

It had been a while since I had the privilege to be in such a splendid showroom. I had a similar experience when I had to wear a gown to the Emmy Awards in 2004 and have had walked a few red carpets. This was also reminiscent of when I worked for Aaron Spelling and Douglas S. Cramer as a teenager and had to help assist the talent on behalf of my bosses with a myriad of things including miscellaneous errands and wardrobe. However, this time around it was for me. These lovely people at Terani Couture were here to help me and that pretty gown was going to be for me to wear and dance in. All that cancer took away and more was slowly trickling back in to my life.

There were ten dresses lined up in the fitting room waiting for me to slip into. They had petite sizes, which not all designers carry, and made it more comfortable for me to wear. Often gowns are made for very tall ladies; Terani Couture keeps in mind that women come in all shapes and sizes. This is something I incorporate into my company too. We have a true people rainbow.

Feelings of inferiority flooded in. *"How could I possibly pull this off?"* I said to myself. Normally, I tend to be fairly confident in my abilities (but more improvement needed). I seldom feel attractive or think that I am. My nose is long with a Roman bridge and turned up at the tip. My eyes are quite large and I have an overbite and half the teeth average adults have. (They were removed at the cancer clinic due to the toxicity in the metal fillings that was overpowering my immune system.) Awkward like a teen in puberty is how I felt. In part the child abuse and cancer had/has tarnished me. The feelings of seeing myself as "used goods" plagued me and an on-going refinement still continued. I'm still a work in progress with flaws and screw ups. I never think my skills make me a better person than others and grateful for all I have.

Jay could tell that I wasn't comfortable. "Enjoy it." He whispered. I nodded my head and shook off the inferiority residue.

Each creation they laid out was more beautiful and glamorous. If I ever felt like a princess, this would be that moment. The designers were wonderful to work with as they provided dresses that flowed and carried through the air like angel's wings. The lighting in the fitting room represented the coloring of the dresses precisely. This is important when photographing.

Helen helped dress me as I tried on all ten gowns and with each one we video recorded me moving in it and doing various leaps and jumps so we could see how the dress would breathe. Lois gave us a lot of coaching of what to look for in narrowing our choices down to five. We had to make sure that any liners under the dresses would not impede my movements and also fit the theme of the book which was: Dance Warrior – Red Ribbons, the second book in my series. Our choices had to fit the victorious message of the book and also give a good representation of me as a dance artist and human being with a flesh heart.

After trying on all the designs, reviewing still snap shots and video playback, we collectively made final decisions and chose the five we felt Lois could work with and that I could dance in unhindered. It was difficult to cast any aside as they were all divine and would work well. Their assistants packed up the gowns in canvass carrying bags and we were on our way to my dad's home via train, bus, and taxi.

My dad was very down to earth. He asked if I was going into the city again tomorrow. He was very curious about what his daughter was doing and no matter how many times I explained it to him, it didn't quite penetrate. I told him I had a photo-shoot with an incredible dance photographer and showed him her website. He pointed his finger at me, "You're going into New York? You're gonna get mugged and raped. You're gonna get mugged, you're gonna get raped, and shot." Jay, my brother, Jane (his wife) and I laughed. He didn't realize how hilarious he was in his delivery but I knew it was his way to say be careful. He then said my hair was too red and that I was going to go bald. I explained to him that it had to be this red so it'd photograph well.

The light source added a hue to it that subdued it more than we wanted for the marketing. In order for it to turn out the tone we wanted for the end result, we had to have it brighter so I used more henna. He didn't get it. He understood the stock market, things of nature, and anything about carpentry, but things like this wasn't his area of interest or expertise. He was the one who grounded me and kept me humble in everyday things. He didn't want his daughter to get a swelled head.

Later that night I set out all the dresses on my bed at his home. I wondered which one Lois would want to use. I loved them all. My sleep schedule was completely turned around and I had to get up rather early for the photo-shoot the next morning. Was this really happening to me?! If someone told me this only two years ago, I would've laughed and thought they were insane. But two years contains over 700 days and over 17,000 hours. A lot can happen in that time if you utilized it well and shaped your dreams into reality.

May 12th was the big day. I had miraculously gotten enough sleep and I felt good. My skin was hydrated, my body limber, and the brain fog cleared somewhat. The surreal moment of meeting Lois was at hand as Jay and I stood in front of her building. We were buzzed in to her Manhattan office, went up the elevator and into her studio. Amazing. We looked around in astonishment. This was the artistry of Lois Greenfield. We had just stepped foot into wonderland. There was some of her photography nestled in various corners of this space, large marque prints from DANCE Magazine covers on the wall. It was very artsy and felt warm like home. There was a space for the shoot that had a white backdrop and all kinds of lighting equipment.

"Hello!" I heard a wonderful spunky voice from behind the front desk. I knew it was Lois as we had a conversation weeks prior on the phone. Lois's head popped up from behind with a huge smile. She stepped out from the desk. She was a petite woman like me but formidable. Kind, soft and strong at the same time. She knows her craft and a master at it. I was greeted with embraces and boy can she hug. I loved this quality in a person and have only been hugged like this one other time in my life. It too was a pivotal moment in my journey.

She had me warm up and take care of myself. Jay joined me as I did the current warm up from my instructor's jazz class. I couldn't think of anything else to do, I was so overwhelmed with the incredibleness of what was happening to me. Lois provided foam rollers and a yoga mat, I was very well taken care of.

She and I went through the dresses and had me catalog them. I tried each one on and quickly modeled them with slight movements just to see how the fabric and gowns would move. They were all lovely. We decided to focus on two particular ones for the actual shoot. One was a white, flowy gown with a goddess-like silhouette. She liked this one because it typified the triumphant message of "Dance Warrior" and what I had survived. Another white dress had many outer layers that were modern looking ruffles. It was amazing but the dress wore me more than I wore it. It wasn't as manageable as another white dress that was similar but with fewer layers of outer fabric. We both chose that one as well.

She had inspirational music playing in the background which added to the mood of the shoot. It's very important to set the right tone. It helps achieve the artistry desired for the final product. Being a dancer, I had to portray "me" as a character and yet keep it very real. Lois was able to bring this out of me and yet still kept me present as myself. Not easy, but she did it with ease.

She wanted me to feel comfortable and I was after I got the nervous butterflies out of me. She also wanted me to move like I move. It wasn't about choreography and it wasn't about staging anything particular. It was about movement and being in the moment. I can't say exactly how she knows how and when to capture these moments in time, but she does. She gets to know her subject and how they move and captures it. Lois's signature look for her photos always finds that moment of breath that differs from all other photographers I've either collaborated with and/or have seen in their portfolios. These moments of breath make sense and tell a story.

This story-telling was an important facet I needed for representing my work on my book cover. I am a story-teller both as an author and dancer-choreographer. Lois completely understood this and she made it happen. We were perfectly matched. It is overwhelmingly joyful to collaborate with a legend.

The next element for the project was adding red ribbons. This is what my dance company was all about: Red Ribbons. It symbolizes love and compassion. It shows how something horrid can be made good. The Mission: Turning darkness into light and celebrating victory over bondage. The book, the dance, the company, it was all tied into a red ribbon. This too Lois understood and was greatly moved by it.

Prior to our shoot, Lois recommended getting various widths, sized, red ribbons. She said get the shiny satin so it'll photograph well. We found 2, 4, 6, and 8-inch width ribbon on spools. Some had wire running through the edges and some not.

At the shoot, after trial and error, we used the 6-inch width ribbon. It was so much fun to experiment and play to see what would "fly" well and work with the message we were attempting to convey. We threw it around me while I moved and she gave great insight to help me stay in the moment. It felt freeing to throw ribbons in the air and move through space collaborating with one of our time's greatest photographers; an artist in her own right.

During the last hour of our shoot I wanted to try something very special. I wore a black dress that was dear to me. Lois was very open to working with my idea. When we started shooting me in this next dress I drew a blank. I froze and couldn't move. I had placed so much stress and pressure on myself wanting to do something perfect for this that I couldn't think. She said "breathe." I smiled knowing that this word meant a lot to me and another person whom I love deeply. I nodded and I danced.

Lois captured me with her lens as I turned and was off-center balance. It was perfect! Lois nailed it and the ribbon performed on cue. The end result was a lot of magic and wonder captured on film in the way only Lois Greenfield can do. What is art if it's not breaking the mold. She breaks the mold.

The movement I did was a turn standing on my right leg with my left leg en passé with right arm overhead and left arm extended to the side. It was a movement that my instructor and I had some intricate and secret communication going on that we shared. I'm not certain what we were saying to one another, but there was some connection occurring. In part it was based on a dream-vision (the one I mentioned earlier) I had about my mom dancing on top of a mountain and a mixture of other interesting things we shared. This particular shot will be on the back cover of my second book: "Dance Warrior - Red Ribbons Shattered Innocence".

We had come to the close of our once in a lifetime session with a renowned artist. I felt I had the better end of the experience but she said I was a beautiful subject and great to work with.

Afterwards, Jay and I ran down 8th Avenue and many more avenues to return the gowns to Terani Couture before they closed at 5:00 pm. Cinderella's coach would turn back into a pumpkin and the fairy tale would then be over.

A migraine had come on fast and furious and I forgot my medication. We ran into a drug store and bought whatever would work. On the glass case below the cash register was a stone that had "Breathe" etched into it. We bought the stone. Things had a way of coming full circle…sort of. There were still a few ribbons left untied. My future with "The b-fly" unknown.

Jay and I had a celebratory pizza pie and took a horse-drawn carriage ride around Central Park and reflected upon what just happened. Jay and I giggled, knowing exactly how hard I had to climb to go from cancer to dancer and then some. We did it. We did it and we still had our horse drawn carriage available to us even after the 5:00 pm deadline.

"Were you nervous?" Jay asked me.

"Yes--" I said without hesitation. I've learned to hide my emotions…most of the time.

"No one would know it." Jay took my hand, "You did it. I'm so proud of you. Now do you believe me when I say that your dreams can come true and that not everything turns out badly?"

I smiled and kissed his forehead. "She should be here with

us." Jay nodded knowingly that I was referencing "The b-fly".

We enjoyed the rest of our stay in NYC, danced at Ailey, and had many adventures. I was asked by my dad before we left to head back to LA. "Where are you going next?" I told him we're headed towards the second star to the right and that I'd be back soon.

So that concludes my tale of how I went from Cancer to Dancer and why I am called a "Dance Warrior". I fight for those I love and for myself. If you're wondering what happened to "The b-fly", what I did with the stone that said "Breathe", my career, and other unanswered questions, please do read the second volume in the "Dance Warrior" Book Series: "Dance Warrior – Red Ribbons Shattered Innocence".

Please know that the second half of your life can be better than your first half. God gave us all talents, that gives you credits and credibility in specific circles/realms. Perhaps it's time for you to use that foundation and springboard off it. I've already seen that paving come to light for myself. Often times God prepares us on a more intimate level then stretches us in the same area that we've been in for a while. He'll then move us outward reaching more hearts. Sometimes using our talents in the same way throughout life and sometimes not. Life is filled with stages and we're cycling quicker through those stages in our times. Time is short. The greatest lie we believe is that we always have more time.

Photo Jay Kenneth © 2015 Be free mon ami!

Whether we know it or not, we are creating an epic dance with our lives. When we're walking we are moving. When we are running we are exploring our space. Life truly is a dance and we create that communication with our bodies.

CONCLUSION ABOUT MY CANCER

At the moment of my last edit of this book, I contemplate how my world has changed from death to life, bleakness to HOPE. I am about to return to Vegas, triumphant as a survivor--THRIVER. I am returning as a dancer-choreographer performing "ROSEWOOD" with my ensemble in a festival. I only wished my mother and Nana were there to see this. They never saw me dance in my adulthood.

The truth is, the battle with this disease will never be over. I have learned not to hold my breath waiting for the time bomb to go off again. Instead I live my life knowing I have overcome. (Remember: Succumb or Overcome) I have defeated my enemy. I am a dance warrior that went from cancer to dancer. I will continue to use my gifts to show that you too can heal the past so that you can have a future and to be a light in the darkness for HOPE. Fight on mighty warriors and use the gifts and talents that you were given to help others fight.

Warriors are noble. Never step on someone to get to where you want to go. Tread lightly always helping others. If you're inspired by someone or something, do not steal, be your own voice not a regurgitation of others. Sometimes where you're going, you cannot take the people you love dearly with you to travel on your road. Sometimes it's not a bad thing. They may not be ready, not able, not worthy, too scared, or will be a hindrance; as hard as it is it is best to lay them down on the ground where they desire to be. Only time will be able to judge their choices.

As I reflect on the past 10 years of my life, never would I have thought I'd be alive, let alone dancing again. I don't know how it happened exactly, or what the "magic moment" was that altered the path of my existence. It wasn't luck, it wasn't sheer will either, it was perhaps a combination of both those things and pain, woundings, suffering, hardships, joy, happiness, patience, commitment, and so many other things that make the canvass and tapestry of me.

To you the precious reader: I implore you to use your wings and fly. You don't know what you're capable of until you take flight. Let the words of my mouth and the meditation of my heart be revealed to you and encourage you to be on your way. Trust that the wind will catch your wings should you grow weary, loving hands will carry you when you cannot walk one step further, and that someone closer than a friend will know just what to say when it is needed when the tears flood.

ABOUT THE AUTHOR – NO, IT'S ABOUT YOU

BY NOELLE ANDRESSEN

I'm pleased to be writing again. Enjoy! My HOPE is that you'll be encouraged and think twice about those whose shoes you don't wear today but could tomorrow. Since this entire book is about the author: me, I don't think more needs to be shared on the topic of "me". It needs to be about you now. Since I am not a resume or my credits, I will just let my life be the testimony to you. If you are interested in my BIO or credits please visit my company website: RubansRougesDance.com

Simply Said: I am not bound by chains, but my roots go deep into fertile ground. I'm just a dancer that likes to tell stories…my true stories so that you too may find HOPE in dark times. I dance my scars to show you that you too can heal. It's the best way I can turn tragedy into triumph. So here's some nourishment for your entire being, but heal your past so that you can have a future.

It took a lot of courage to get to this point to bare my soul.

ENCOURAGEMENT FOR YOUR SOUL
INSPIRATIONAL NOTES

Get your paint brush – Get your paints – Create a beautiful life.

If you were to see your life as a work of art; how much more care and detail would you apply to it. Life is like a dance. Sometimes it's slow, sometimes it's fast…but whatever you do, keep moving. Persevere and keep focused. Your life depends on it. Please know there is no need to go it alone. There are people who love you and who are ready to give you much needed support. There are even more, many more than you can possibly imagine. People who CAN love you if you give them a chance. You were molded and created. Every molecule of your being is precious. You are not an accident. You have purpose. You were wroth the while. You were worth the risk. You were worth the wait.

Let the hand held heart guide you to your purpose. Those who have beautiful souls will resonate: peace, patience, kindness, thoughtfulness, commitment, generosity, and above all LOVE. The rose will always bloom in adversity. It's okay to cry. Roses do cry when their petals are torn. The truth beneath the rose is that the rose always points upwards from which the sun's love and rays shine down. When you look deep within only pure love filters through the rose's roots….it is the secret of The Silent Rose.

Something to ponder: how can we be racist when we're all part of the same race ~ the human race…love equally

Learn to let go of your past (not of the goodness in that past, retain that for it makes you whole.) Not all tears are evil or evilly intended. Keep breathing and reject the horrors that would weigh you down. Be at peace with yourself. Create a future with a legacy of goodness. It is not beyond your grasp no matter how daunting or insurmountable it may seem to you. One step at a time. One breath at a time. One smile at a time. Trust in wings and trust in the breath that blows the petals on the wind. The butterfly needs the rose just as much as the rose needs the butterfly. Vibrant petals and Mighty wings…It was the testing of time that made them both more beautiful. Vibrant were her petals and Mighty were her wings. Change your legacy: Use your wings.

If you see someone in need: use your wings. If you see someone hurting: use your wings. If you find yourself feeling low: use your wings. Once you have your wings you can never lose them.

Never forget the sign of the butterfly. When in doubt just remember the signs brought to you to gird you up and carry you forward like the gentle breezes.

Emerge from you chrysalis of fear so that you may become the beautiful creation you were meant to be.

The sky is always blue and the sun is always shining. Above all the darkness light is always there. Sometimes holding on does more damage than letting go; what if there's someone on the other end? Be wise before you move on what if you were on the other end?

How high does one need to leap to reach their star? Sweet babe, you must leap as high as necessary. There is a HOPE that transcends despair. It will lift your soul if you trust in it. Believe so you can be free to breathe. Do not give up! Your star is waiting for you. Strive for your personal best. Being number one is a lonely illusion. There's room for everybody so be open to many hearts. Labels are for clothes not people. Compete with yourself and do not compete against others. Seldom can people compete against others without jealousy, anger, fear, wrongful desire, and plotting seeping in. You'll be much happier and less stressed and you'll draw more people to you. You can improve without this type of competing; it's called discipline and that trait brings more good fruit into your life.

It's about being content and so self-confident that you have nothing to prove except to yourself. Remember that one good deed can shift the balance of the world. Don't forget to show kindness to others. Love is more than feelings. It is a commitment that is expressed with our actions and deeds towards others.

Speak of love, it will nourish other's souls. Give love, it will nourish yours. Yes, there is something that revives my soul, it is the soft droplets of water that reaches the depths within. Like pure innocence filled with wonder, the majesty and cleansing power that makes all things new again. You were not meant for destruction. There's a beautiful plan for your life. In all things: be a vessel of love. If you were to see your life as a work of art, how much more care and detail would you apply to it.

If someone scars you; make it your crowning glory. Rise above your wounds and use them as a beautiful garland around your head to say "I have overcome!"

ACT THREE - My Last Battleground (c) 2012

There always comes a time when the protagonist in Act Three must make a "Decision" -- a big one. To stand and fight the antagonist (the shark, the storm, nature, society, himself, a disease, etc.) or put his tail between his legs-turn around-pee his pants-run away-and forget that all this horrible stuff ever happened to him (or her). Alright, in most great films we seldom ever see that...urine stream, but you get what I'm speaking of, yes?

However, the French New Wave of film making didn't always end things on the positive note nor with closure or with an ending for that matter--but it was an exciting time in film making...aside from these examples, a great percentage of films has our protagonist fighting bravely and either winning to tell the tale or sacrificing himself for a greater cause which is still a triumphant WIN!

This last ACT--Act Three is the protagonist's Last Battleground. He decides he's going to stand no matter what. He decides he's going to do what he set out to do without regret and do it wholeheartedly. He has the resolve to do what it takes to finish what he started...but how did our hero get to this point? As I'm approaching the one year anniversary of my mother's death I can't help but reflect upon this: CANCER. I also am curious as to my own resolve as to how I chose to fight My ACT THREE and My Last Battleground, why God allowed me to survive, what was my future purpose once I survived (obviously I THRIVED--but that isn't and wasn't the notion at the time--trust me on this one.

As your head is bent over a barf bowl wondering if the nausea will ever pass, the last thing on your mind is future purpose. I just wanted to stop barfing--GOAL NUMBER ONE!)The men folk around me have helped me formulate this essay because memories are funny--we all have them and we can experience the same one but recall our part or our viewpoint differently. WHAT IT WAS *in brief digression & to catch up those unknowing (I have other writings about this journey elsewhere)* My diagnosis came suddenly but not as a surprise.

I'd had other health issues to deal with in the past, ones that threatened my life but they were dealt with as well. Cancer had at that time already shown its ugly face in my family in the women-- these women were strong too--make no mistake about that because they had kahonahs just like me--make no mistake or mistaken my kindness for weakness. I'm just a nice person with a lot of patience until given reason otherwise. I knew it was a matter of time for me; just one of those things being a human being you can sense and also see the logic and reason of the genetic and environmental connections...a "no brainer" since my family all lived within 3 blocks of one another in Vegas. Say hello to 55 miles north-ish of Vegas: Yucca Mountain = nuke testing. A very high level of radiation does cause our bodies to be predisposed to cancer-FACT!

Plus perchlorate (used to make rocket fuel) was in our drinking water which they never filtered out (?) Vegas has one of the highest cancer rates. Look at the stats. Then look at my blood tests, mammograms, etc. I was a stat waiting to happen. I chose an alternate therapy because I still think that traditional medicine is what did my grandmother in. I wanted to choose another way that would give my body a fighting chance and my red blood cells the ability to rebuild. I did a lot of research on this--I don't regret my choices. Those close to me thought I was crazy for doing so and some pushed me away and disowned me calling me selfish. My attitude was: it's my body--MY choice. Plus when you're looking at possibly dying--you have the right to be selfish to save it. Gotta love those types.

Third Derailment - I see each of the 3 derailments as three separate acts in my life, or chapters, or portions, or segments, or use whatever word suits your fancy. It's all good. I'm a writer and love to use metaphors, hyperbole, analogies, and alliterations to make a point. Okay, so cancer put a sudden stop to things again...this would be the third derailment of my dancing. Tedious, yes. But again, it would pose this challenge to me: are you up for it? What do you want from your life? just as an aside because there's some unfounded confusion....I didn't start dancing nor training or performing/dancing in 2007. I had this whole entire life long before what many in LA know me as. My life didn't start when I first met anyone in 2007; neither did my dancing.

No disrespect, especially to my current mentors/teachers /trainers, but it's truth. I started ballet at 4, I did dancing, choreography, performing and all of that I do now when I was very young. I trained on and off because of derailments out of my control. But when I trained it was full time and serious. I wasn't born a dancer, or a singer, or a musician, there were years of work and training behind all of that and most of you didn't see it but it happened.

MY THIRD ACT - 2007 was the beginning of my THIRD ACT. I was presented with this choice to make: Stand and fight or run away. Not from my battle with cancer or the pre-cancer that soon followed...it was for the aftermath of cancer and the ominous choice succinctly put in an old adage: "I'll become bitter or I'll become better." Bottom line with that stuff--just sayin' you have two choices with that.

As for me my attitude was: Screw being bitter--that only hurts yourself and those you love most, so really what choice does one truly have logically speaking. I chose to become better. And mind you, not just a better dancer--more importantly a better person. But boy did I have a lot of work to do physically. I was only trying to get back into some kind of "shape". What I was unprepared for was that I would become a dancer again. A different type of dancer. I chose to fight and rebuild my body painstakingly so. It's taken some time as its 6 years later, but it's been worth it all. Cancer does a number on your brain as well and so does the treatment.

Hundreds of hours training, many nights of dealing with aftermath symptoms, a recurrence of the disease, a fragile immune system, etc....It was a literal and physical re-birth from the feet up. So those who've had me in their classes, do you now understand why I just couldn't bounce off the walls and do what everyone else did immediately? I was 90 pounds and only 18 months out of my treatment. No one would ever suspect any of this now except I say it to be so.

There needs to be grace and graciousness given to someone not just me but anyone who's fought for their lives won and is standing firm to claim back that which was stolen from them (not attacked).In 2007 I chose to just throw all of what I knew away. I was a different person. I was going to start with a clean slate and re-learn everything. I had no choice in some respect because my brain was badly besieged with chemicals and bi-products of the treatment I had. It doesn't matter what route you choose to healing--it all stinks and it all leaves scars of some sort.

I was a damaged BUT VERY STRONG person. I emphasize that because not only myself but others who've had to go through physical issues have been stigmatized. This is wrong and I'm fighting it on my behalf and others like me. Please know that the moment you judge someone, quickly put yourself in their shoes.

Cancer strikes 1 in 8 and then 1 in 4 after age 50. So your chances of cancer are high and you may read this and take it in somberly and respectfully or you may not. You may also find yourself a few years from now reflecting on your reaction to my words as you're hearing your diagnosis (god forbid -- of course I don't wish it on anyone). But words to the wise: be careful how you judge for you may get a chance to walk that path. Learn from my mistake, yes? So...this is where I'm at right now. My Third Act.

This is the point in my life where I chose to stand and fight. I had always thought it was on my death bed in another country while getting my treatment that I made this "Third Act Decision". That was only the beginning. Yes I did ask God and bargain with Him (if you can call it that), that I wanted to reach many and give them hope if He would spare my life. He spared my life and now I use my dancing to reach others to give them HOPE.HOPE that you can: Not only survive child molestation, cancer, a broken heart, a broken body, abuse, neglect, shame, guilt, but THRIVE and know what it is to be whole on the other side.

The biggest difference for me now is that I'm using my talents to help others and not lift myself up. Amazing what a life threatening/altering instance (and a run-in with God) can do to transform a person ;o)SO please when you see my pieces and they strike a chord, let it make beautiful music within your heart and not a chord of bitterness for I'm only the messenger bringing HOPE.

Do not become offended should my art reach and touch you in a way you don't desire--I don't know your story and I'm not to blame, I only know my story and want to share it. If I can survive to THRIVE so can you. Please listen to these words: I've been there and I'm on your side. We are part of the same exact race: The Human Race - we are connected.

December 14, 2012 ·

Wow, Jay was watching me type this and he just said bluntly:
"I know why she had to die from cancer this way...
if she lived any longer she would've done something even more reckless than she had done previously like skydive, rode a boat during a hurricane, etc. (She was always reckless), if she would've kept doing this she would've ended up dying instantly doing something reckless and not be able to think about the lord and eternity. It was the fact that she had to be in a sick bed and think about her soul and eternity that changed her heart."

It took her death to give her life: ETERNAL LIFE. She may have realized that God has been knocking on her heart for decades using me, my brother, Jay, Kris and so many others. He had to have her still and he spared her much physical suffering.

It was cancer that killed her body but saved her soul.........it gave her time to think about her life after her death; for she knew she was dying and knew it was a matter of time. Her decaying and still body caused her to think about everything. These types of situations often do cause us to dwell upon things and consider what happens when we die. I know in the still moments she did accept Jesus into her heart. I know this because when I first accepted Christ on my wedding day February 10th (a very blessed day for me in many ways) I feared for my mom's soul. The realization of how we all must face our mortality hit me hard. I heard the lord's voice whisper in my ear: "She'll know me upon her death bed." I just didn't think that death bed would happen until she was well into her 80s. But god also told me that things were going to go super-fast once Nana died.

She had asked my brother what he believed 6 weeks before she was diagnosed with anything. she already knew where I stood. She knew my convictions in the lord Christ Jesus and salvation through him. I was told to keep my mouth shut and not "upset" her with my religion. Well it didn't stop god from reaching her heart in the quiet moments. No one can undo the eternal. She's finally safe in the hands of god, seeing my baby girl (and lord knows how many other of my miscarried babies--i truly don't understand when a soul is placed inside a human being), being with her mom-my Nana. I was promised that all in my blood line would be saved. And one special heart that is very much like family and may as well be considered in my blood line. I must stand on these truths. These truths that cannot be proven except by the hearts of the righteous that have ears to listen to the lord's commands.

Okay, so maybe that answers one question. But why couldn't I have more time with her? I'm left to know in my heart that God does things that none of us will ever completely understand. I have to reconcile this and accept that it was for the good of his perfect will. I don't like that he allows suffering in this world, it's still a difficult thing for me to fathom, but he allows it all for reasons unknown to me but not unknown to him. I don't claim to know or understand the answers.

Many believe we are in the end days or on the cusp of it. I don't pretend to know the answers for this either. I'm right there with you questioning and seeking truth. Our world is falling apart ferociously quick. With that notion many believe we are called to do more than our predecessors. Also, many believe these things will happen and needs to happen so that certain things are fulfilled. God commands us to firstly love Him then our neighbor as ourselves. Our main job is drawing souls to God and LOVE. Being vessels for God and as the days shorten; the work is plentiful; the workers are few.

We do not have the luxury our predecessors had by having one job or career and touching lives on the fringe. Now is the time to be utilized through a career by God and reach hearts exponentially. Time to go in deeper and claim God's harvest of love not for our own but as His helpers. Farmer's hands get sore, calloused, and dirty during this process of a beautiful harvest. It is hard work, but necessary with few willing to do the work. Time is short beloveds. Aggressively short. Planning 401k's, retirement, etc was something for our grandparents and some of our parents. They had securities. Many are seeing these old ways fail. Perhaps we need soul planning more than retirement planning?

Who will say: God send me to reach the broken hearted? Who will love the least of these? He will reap through us if we are willing. It's God's job to use our talents through us. It's our job to be obedient to God. Let God expand these words for you.

I think Jay shares the gift of knowledge that I have as well. Thank you lord for putting my heart at ease somewhat...however now, now I fear for another soul. Be gracious and gentle lord with this one precious heart, please, I implore you. Lead her gently.

DANCE WARRIOR - FROM CANCER TO DANCER

COMING SOON
DANCE WARRIOR – RED RIBBONS
SHATTERED INNOCENCE

Please enjoy this excerpt of my upcoming book, due out this year. It tells the tale of my sexual child abuse, the lives I touched, my healing and victory. The triumph awaits you!

"LIL GIRL"
Written by Noelle Andressen © 2012

A lil girl who loved her mom would always help her by: carrying in groceries, keeping things neat & if the mom was sweeping the floor she'd get on her hands & knees & help with that too. The mom would watch the lil girl work hard and help but would only respond by rolling her eyes at her. The lil girl had many sisters. The other sisters wouldn't dream of helping the mom at all as it was beneath them but the mom encouraged this behavior. The lil girl was treated as an outcast—she was a scape-goat.

Many times the lil girl would see a deep sorrow in her mom and would smile at her & try to get her to laugh, but seldom would the mom acknowledge her. If the mom laughed it was only to laugh at her in mockery not with her in joy; and a smile cast the mom's way would be rewarded with contempt and disdain. The lil girl would feel the sting of rejection and disapproval but still kept smiling.

The lil girl often wondered why whenever she'd do something kind 4 her mom, her mom would never show approval or thank her. The mom would always thank the other sisters for doing lesser things, but never encourage or acknowledge her—especially not in public; for the mom had too much pride to even speak the girl's name.

The lil girl had a name…a beautiful name, but the mom would never call her by her name only her sisters. This hurt the lil girl coz she loved her mom more than the others & showed it through actions. She couldn't understand what she'd done to deserve this dehumanizing treatment. If mom would say my name it'd show that she loved me.

To hide the pain of rejection the lil girl would dance. She danced & danced until her toes were sore. Any time the mom would see the lil girl dance, she'd quickly turn her head & walk away. She knew that the lil girl was very good--the lil girl had a special gift but the mom couldn't and wouldn't admit it verbally. The mom's heart was very hard like a cold relic that showed its age with deep crevices of bitterness--anger. The mom's true inner beauty that once was suffocated by resentment, regret, greed, hatred, envy, fear and rage.

One day the lil girl decided to make a beautiful dance for her mom & felt that she could touch her heart & connect this way..."Maybe a dance would break through the stone cold heart?" The lil girl remembered that her mom used to dance when she was younger & thought she was a beautiful dancer. The lil girl never knew why the mom stopped dancing...watching her mom dance gave her such inspiration, peace & joy! The mom was so beautiful when she danced.

The lil girl finished the dance and was able to convince her mom to watch her. At first as the lil girl began to dance the mom sat upright and staunch in her wing-back chair; ready to pass judgment. But as the lil girl continued to move so beautifully the mom's erect posture softened and she leaned in and rested her palms on her knees. The lil girl was not only a wonderful dancer, but her inner light shone so brightly on the outside. It was infectious--it was radiant--it was pure love. This is what made the lil girl's dancing even more moving--this is what seeped in to the mom's hardened heart.

There was a particular simple gesture with the palms the lil girl made; the mom repeated the palm gesture as she was greatly moved by it. She became so engrossed in the dance that a smile slipped out unbeknownst to the lil girl. If the lil girl could have seen the mom's face, she would've noticed that the smile was genuine and it made the mom's radiance and beauty break through the crevices of the hardened shell around her heart. There was still something alive underneath all that darkness and hardened shell.

The core somehow remained intact in the mom and the lil girl was able to touch it and reach it.

The lil girl had danced her best and finished and bowed her head. The mom quickly composed herself as she noticed she was completely enraptured by her daughter. She resumed her erect posture and the smile was wiped from her face. The lil girl looked up at her mom and had such hope that at least perhaps her name would be said. The lil girl placed a red rose in her mom's hand. "I couldn't have done it without you."

The mom was speechless as she truly was moved like never before--impressed beyond words but couldn't bring herself to be honest, to be vulnerable, to be human. This would show weakness—that wasn't tolerated in her upbringing. Emotions were considered "taboo" and to show and express them would result in discipline. The mom hid her true inner feelings and shielded her heart and let the stone interior reflect the exterior.

The lil girl looked for some sign that the mom's heart was reached but found none. Remember the lil girl was dancing and didn't see how the mom was truly moved. This is such a tragedy as it would've been a "sign" to the lil girl.

The mom got up, left the room & closed the door. Heartbroken was the lil girl & up went a huge wall around this precious one's heart. No one in—no one out. Hate choked out the love she had. She now hardened her heart like her mom. But on the other side of the door where the lil girl couldn't see her mom; the mom was shedding tears, real tears as she embraced the rose. The mom then repeated the palm gesture from the lil girl's dance.

Time had passed & the lil girl was now grown up & a beautiful dancer on stage. One evening at the end of a performance, as the adult lil girl took her bow, she saw her mom in the front row with a red rose. The adult lil girl turned her gaze away. Back stage the mom approached her daughter.

With all the courage & strength she could gather, the adult lil girl walked to her mom. The mom handed her the red rose. The lil girl held the rose in her hand and could feel the anger travel from her heart to her palm. Her fingers tensed slightly and were very tempted to crush the rose. The adult lil girl said: "I thought u hated me."

The mom said, "No, I hated myself." The mom let the lil girl see a genuine tear fall from her eyes. "You see we're so much alike and it should've given me great comfort to know that I had a friend that would always understand me but instead I was hateful. You reminded me of the person I could've been & how I failed to live up to that. I'm so ashamed how I treated you. You didn't deserve it."

The mom made the palm gesture from the lil girl's dance. The mom emotionally broke and embraced the lil girl and cried like a dam bursting forth with deep waters of regret and repentance.

The lil girl still had the rose in her hand and was very tempted to give in to the position of emotional power she had at the moment. The mom was in a weak place and the lil girl could've lashed out with intense rage and repay all the evil and abuse that was inflicted upon her by her mom and could've destroyed her. Her fingers clasped harder and were about to crush the rose...

"I've always loved you..." trickled from the mom's lips. With those words, the lil girl embraced her mom.

To conclude this story, the mom said the lil girl's name & things were healed as they both had something within them that remained somehow intact: TRUE LOVE.

Ms. Andressen at 4 years old and in her 30s.

TRUE LOVE STOPS THE CYCLE OF ABUSE.

What was the lil girl's name?...I know it & so do you. This lil girl's name is your name, it's my name...meaning, I think we've all gone through something similar to this or at least know someone who has. This lil girl could've been you or me or anyone. The mom herself was abused physically, emotionally, mentally, as a child and couldn't and didn't deal with it as an adult so she passed it on to her daughter. Because of the mom's self-loathing, she singled out the one daughter who had the most sensitive heart and who loved her the most; she knew she was the closest to her.

What I have to say about all this: we need to be careful how we treat people. Our own little issues can be hurtful to others and become big issues unintentionally. So if you have issues take this little story as a motivator to change. Remember that your issues are yours to own not to put on someone else; although if you need help do ask. It's never too late! There's always a fear of change, but I believe the fear of staying the same is even greater. I always opt for change and it gets easier the more I do it. Plus you'll be quite surprised how much graciousness is in people's hearts to forgive.

While there are many layers to this parable & tons of psychological themes of self-loathing, jealousy, etc..., take from it what you will, just remember we're frail human beings. I was asked to repost this by many of you so here it is. I don't want to say that I hope you enjoy it, because it's not enjoyable—it's very sad. But perhaps this will help open some eyes that need to see and ears that need to hear. And most importantly don't let any person (abusive or not) take away your beauty.

In homage to Cunningham and Graham.

STAY IN TOUCH AND IN THE KNOW WITH MS. NOELLE ANDRESSEN'S WORK AND HER PROJECTS

Find out when Ms Andressen & her dance company will be performing in your area. Be sure to sign up for our email blasts for special discounts on tickets for these performances as well. We'll often update and add book signing events and tours across the country. If you'd like to make a request for her to speak at your event or visit your bookstore, please get in touch with our Executive Director. That information is on line at our website.

Ms. Andressen does Facebook LIVE at least once a month. Be sure to catch her broadcasts. Our schedules are posted on our social media. Thank You! Because of You we are able to bring incredible "Dance Drama" performances that allows you the audience member to "Feel the Experience"™

To make a donation to our non-profit organization, please check on line and donate via ssl server or by phoning our office.

OTHER WAYS TO HELP & SUPPORT US
Visit our social media pages below.
Share our information with your family & friends.
Become an active member on our forum pages & blogs.
Contribute and share your experiences with us.
Purchase tickets to our shows.
Buy these books for your friends & family.

WEBSITE: www.RubansRougesDance.com
FACEBOOK: www.facebook.com/RubansRougesDance
www.facebook.com/NoelleAndressenDancer
INSTAGRAM: Rubans_Rouges_Dance
PINTEREST: NoelleRose5678
TWITTER: RUBANSROUGES
YouTube: www.youtube.com/redribbonsdance

www.ingramcontent.com/pod-product-compliance
Lightning Source LLC
Chambersburg PA
CBHW050548160426
43199CB00015B/2578